How to Save
THE
CONSTITUTION

How to Save

THE
CONSTITUTION

Restoring the Principles of Liberty

PAUL B. SKOUSEN

&

W. CLEON SKOUSEN

IZZARD INK
PUBLISHING

IZZARD INK PUBLISHING COMPANY
PO Box 522251
Salt Lake City, Utah 84152
www.izzardink.com

LIBRARY OF CONGRESS CONTROL NUMBER: 2019931761

Designed by Alissa Rose Theodor
Cover Design by Andrea Ho
Illustrations by Zach Meyer
Cover Images: Lukas Gojda/Shutterstock.com Color Symphony/Shutterstock.com

First Edition September 17, 2019

Contact the author at info@paulskousen.com

Hardback ISBN: 978-1-64228-052-4
Paperback ISBN: 978-1-69381-259-0
eBook ISBN: 978-1-64228-050-0

Freedom is Fragile

James Madison
September 28, 1820

"I believe there are more instances of the abridgment of the freedom of the people by gradual and silent encroachments of those in power than by violent and sudden usurpations."

Abraham Lincoln
September 17, 1859

"The people of these United States are the rightful masters of both Congresses and courts, not to overthrow the Constitution but to overthrow the men who pervert it."

Ronald Reagan
January 5, 1967

"Freedom is a fragile thing and is never more than one generation away from extinction. It is not ours by inheritance; it must be fought for and defended constantly by each generation, for it comes only once to a people. Those who have known freedom and then lost it have never known it again."[1]

THE FOUNDING FATHERS'
BOOK OF INSTRUCTIONS

Several of the Framers who helped create the Constitution often spoke of wonderful moments when brilliant ideas, concepts, and principles of self-government crystallized in their minds. John Adams, George Washington, James Madison, Thomas Jefferson, Benjamin Franklin, and certain others were especially active in documenting these insights in their letters and speeches.

Unfortunately, no formal collection of those epiphanies was ever published. If it ever is, the book's name should be *The Founding Fathers' Book of Instructions*. "Instructions" because these insights anticipate a time when America might lose its way and need immediate help. Such instructions would serve to re-establish the inspired ideas that could save the nation from ruin. They could be utilized as an action plan, a set of requirements, a path forward at a time when liberty was on the brink of ruin, and the people needed direction.

In the pages that follow is the essence of *The Founding Fathers' Book of Instructions*:

1. The 28 great ideas that make true liberty possible.
2. The four pillars upon which self-government stands.
3. The Moral Code that is inextricably essential to liberty.
4. Economic Liberty whereby tangible proof of living by true principles is created and enjoyed.

5. The role of Virtue in sustaining liberty.
6. The role of Personal Responsibility in perpetuating liberty.

Should the American people ever stumble and put their liberties at risk, the Founders firmly believed there was always a divine or manifest destiny that ensured the rescue of America, causing it to rise, Phoenix-like, from the ashes.[2]

The Founding Fathers' Book of Instructions leads Americans through the seven steps that are essential to that Phoenix moment. Those seven steps comprise a pathway that we will follow in our personal search for the restoration of America.

CONTENTS

CONTENTS

FOREWORD

By Fred G. Clark

he American giant towers over the world in its physical strength, greater than that of all the rest of the nations put together.[3]

But something is wrong with America.

At this high moment of history when the task of world leadership has been thrust upon us, we stand confused, reluctant, hesitant, and ineffectual.

We are no longer certain what we stand for, and this, I believe, is because we have forgotten the circumstances surrounding the birth of our nation. . . .

For decades it has been popular in America for the cynical intellectuals to sneer and scoff at what we call the traditions of Americanism.

The instruments of this sabotage are words and thoughts — plausible half-truths, sly appeals to that spark of larceny that lurks in every human heart, subtle suggestions of an atheistic nature, and the careful nurturing of a patronizing attitude toward everything America has held to be fine and sacred.

The people who planted these words and thoughts may have been either stupid or vicious, fools or foreign agents, smart-alecks, or cunning organizers.

What they were does not now matter—the thing that does matter is to counteract what they have done.

Everybody in every position of leadership has to get into this act because the damage has affected every phase of our lives.

The places in which this sabotage occurred were the schools, the churches, the communist-dominated labor halls, the lecture platforms, the motion pictures, the stage, the pages of our newspapers and magazines, and the radio. Every means of communication has been utilized against us. . . .

The man (or nation) who has a plan—a way of life—in which he believes, has mental security.

To destroy this security, one must destroy that man's faith in his plan.

Reliance on a code of life which, if held in common with one's fellow men, brings peace of mind, develops the abilities of the group. . . .

The degree to which the American code of life has been weakened can best be demonstrated by simply calling attention to the degree to which the foundation of that code has been weakened.

Many people become self-conscious when discussing this foundation: I am not one of those people.

That foundation (and of this there cannot be the slightest shadow of a doubt) is made up of the Ten Commandments and the Golden Rule.

Within this moral code, we have a complete way of life.

Acceptance of these precepts takes care of every phase of human life—spiritual, political, social, and economic. . . .

America was a nation of people who had faith in their political and economic systems because they had faith in God, and had built those systems around the teachings of God.

Every collectivist from Karl Marx to Stalin has agreed that faith in God must be destroyed before socialism can take over.

Therefore, it was obvious that the problem of sabotaging America's faith in America was the problem of transferring the people's faith in God to faith in the State.

That thing called morality in politics, business, and private contracts, had to be broken down.

To an increasing extent the American people have come to look upon morality as an old-fashioned superstition.

Religion has for many church members become a safe way of dying rather than a good way of living. . . .

There are many who tell us that all this is a waste of time—that the process of socialism cannot be reversed; that once it is started it must run its course.

This we do not believe—we consider it part of the fake propaganda that is poisoning our will to resist.

Our first-hand experience with millions of typical Americans convinces us that there is nothing wrong with America that the truth will not correct.

We must be militant.

We are no longer fighting to defend a way of life—we are fighting to get it back.

Our problem is a counterrevolution.

In this fight we are not going to get any important help from any political party—the politicians have been giving the people the kind of government the people say they want, and the policies in Washington will not change until the people change.

And that is the job of people who know the truth and love it enough to spread it.

This must be a crusade—the greatest crusade in history.

Those who take part are called hard names—reactionaries, Fascists, professional patriots, apologists for special privilege, and many others.

These smears are also a part of the enemy's strategy.

Our forefathers who fought the first revolution were also smeared.

They too were told that they were wasting their time and their fortunes on a hopeless adventure. It would have been much easier for them to go along with the established order and try in some way or other to buy their freedom instead of fighting for it.

But unlike many people today, they preferred to fight.

How many people do you know today who are sitting back, confident that their bank accounts will in one way or another protect them and their families from the creeping tyranny of strong central government?

That is what people [in pre-World War II] thought in Italy, in Germany, in New Zealand, in Australia, and still later, in England.

All they did was put off the hour of decision and weaken their power to fight back.

In America people now console themselves with the idea that it can never happen here.

It seems to them unreal that people with good old-fashioned American names and fine-looking American faces could exercise the tyrannies that have always been identified with bombs, daggers, whiskers, and unpronounceable syllables.

But the fact remains that it is already beginning.

Most of the instruments of tyranny are already on the statute books. The means of freedom's destruction are already in the hands of the Federal administration.

You say that no administration would dare use them?

All history is against that answer—in the long run, power corrupts, and absolute power corrupts absolutely.

It always has and it always will.

Our best weapon is truth—we must start using it.

And we must do it while there is still time.

INTRODUCTION

Does the Constitution Need to be Saved?

The abundance of evidence pointing to a Constitution in trouble is carefully itemized in hundreds of books, thousands of articles, and millions of words, all of them pointing to political corruption, dishonesty, confusion, and activism in both major parties at the highest levels of government. A sound and respected Constitution served to prevent this kind of power-mongering from taking hold, but once the people began pushing the Constitution aside as minimally relevant, the Constitution itself began teetering on the verge of destruction.

Can it be Saved?

Missing from this abundance of evidence, however, are clear-cut directions pointing the American people onto the right path to return their founding document to its rightful station.

Saving the Constitution is not as simple as having the right president in The White House, the right legislation passing through Congress, or the right people sitting on the Supreme Court. Its salvation will come from a power that is more intimate, less known, and hardly expected by most Americans.

To that end, this essay is an unapologetic handbook of positive steps to save the Constitution as it was originally intended. It requires from its readers the absorption of a little knowledge, some sincere personal change, and a measure of determined action.

Unfortunately, the formula that follows won't resonate with many Americans. Those who aren't aware of America's serious problems will just ignore it. To others, the necessary course correction will be discredited as absurd. They will destroy it with dismissive mockery, derision, name calling, or scornful rejection, declaring that "It's so narrow and old fashioned, we're enlightened now," to justify today's downward spiral.

And then there are those few, those Americans who recognize that our Constitution is losing its power and relevance. These Americans will find herein a set of instructions on how to save the Constitution. It is for them that this text has been prepared.

Innocent Ignorance is Killing America

For the past dozen decades, the United States as a system of free will and the protection of rights has shed piece by piece the armor that protects human rights and self-government. And, it has been systematically ingesting the elements of corruption.

With each freedom lost, the rising generation assumes the status quo to be the established norm and fails to realize that what once existed has been lost or rendered meaningless.

The Danger of Unchallenged Precedents

Thomas Jefferson warned that "A departure from principle in one instance becomes a precedent for a second; that second for a third; and so on, till the bulk of the society is reduced to mere automatons of misery, to have no sensibilities left but for sin and suffering."[4]

Alexander Hamilton described that erosion, saying "Nothing is more common than for a free people, in times of heat and violence, to gratify momentary passions, by letting into the government, principles and precedents which afterwards prove fatal to themselves."[5]

For lack of perspective, that rising generation is doing little or nothing to correct the losses. Decades of such erosion have brought millions of Americans to their present state of apathy, fear, desperation, and dependence on the government that from the very beginning was never intended and was painfully avoided.

Putting up with "The Way Things Are"

In the second paragraph of the Declaration of Independence, Thomas Jefferson expressed this modern-day decline in these words: "All experience hath shewn," he said, "that mankind are more disposed to suffer, while evils are sufferable, than to right themselves by abolishing the forms to which they are accustomed."[6]

It is an apt description of modern America where tens of millions of citizens are willing to suffer the loss of freedoms so long as they get the material essentials they deem necessary for a productive life.

Most Americans sense that an erosion of rights has been occurring, and that something is terribly wrong, but they can't pinpoint the exact problem. They flail about their power to vote in hopes of hitting upon the right fix, but year after year the nation fails to reach the core root of what ails it.

The Constitution is not Enough

The call to save the Constitution is not complete without a call to save the human attitude necessary to sustain self-government. It's not simply an exercise of returning to those original words in the Constitution. The national culture must also be restored.

"Too often in recent years, patriotic symbols have been shunted aside," said FBI Director J. Edgar Hoover in 1962. "Our national heroes have been maligned, our history distorted. Has it become a disgrace to pledge allegiance to our flag—or to sign a loyalty oath, or pay tribute to our national anthem? Is it shameful to encourage our children to memorize the stirring words of the men of '76? Is it becoming opprobrious [offensive] to state 'In God we trust' when proclaiming our love of country?[7] ...Every strong nation in history has lived by an ideal and has died when its ideals were dissipated ...The nation which honors God is protected and strengthened by Him."[8]

In the face of such decline, Jefferson declared the solution is to replace a government that has stopped serving the people: "It is their right, it is their duty," he said, "to throw off such Government, and to provide new Guards for their future security."[9]

Confronting the Dark Side of Affluence

For today, throwing off such Government to provide new Guards is not overthrowing a king and parliament as it was for the Founding Generation in 1776. It is for us a different kind of work. Ours is to throw off corruption.

Our challenges are great:

- We as a people have corrupted ourselves, claiming corruption to be a constitutional right while rejecting the personal responsibilities permanently yoked to each of those constitutional rights.
- We have lost much of that binding glue of patriotism, that wonderful unifying determination to protect and prosper the country.
- We have stumbled into that mindset of the prideful, believing that we are above traditional and proven values; that the life we know today in America is impervious to destruction; that those working to keep alive traditional values are stifled, rigid, and homespun; that religious or law-abiding people are sadly shackled to an old way of life that was gladly jettisoned for a more relaxed, tolerant culture.
- We are losing that awareness of America's divine destiny and the people's sacred allegiance to that great purpose that motivated millions to proudly fight and die to defend, preserve, and protect our beloved United States of America.
- We are divided along almost every social front, waging war with each other over politics, patriotism, religion, race, morals, gender, incomes, values, and virtues. Ambitious agitators and malcontents stir up our people to divide them, separate them,

and weaken them. Standing up for a personal opinion can cost people their jobs, a penalty, a position, peer respect, equal protection under the law, and even their freedom.

Restore, Save, Strengthen

The way back to a restored Constitution is marked by a very real change in our personal lives. Like seeds cast in good soil, great leaders will grow from individuals, families, and communities practicing correct principles. Regardless of where the voices of destruction might eventually lead America, when the day is done, traditional values will ultimately rise above the ruins to reign supreme.

"We have a restoration job on our hands," wrote Leonard E. Read in 1962. "Freedom must experience a rebirth in America; that is, we must re-establish it from fundamental principles." [10]

Natural Principles and Laws Don't Change

In the pages that follow are these fundamental principles that have been passed down to modern America. Studying them makes it clear that America's greatest problems are not because the Constitution has failed to keep up with the times as some people claim. We suffer because those principles have become largely ignored, neglected, or intentionally rejected.

America's biggest challenge for saving the Constitution really boils down to something quite simple: Where do we begin?

A wise ecclesiastical leader long ago once made a promise that has proven itself of inestimable value time and again. It's just as applicable today as it was almost a hundred years ago. He wisely counseled, "Just start and the way will be opened." [11]

Just start. It's direct, it's simple, it's the key to all of America's forward motion. It's something that we can put to work right here, right now.

From one grateful American to another, let's put that promise to the test. Let's just start. Let's go save our Constitution.

STEP 1

WHO? WHAT? WHEN? WHERE? WHY? HOW?

Learn the answers to the six questions that are essential to saving the Constitution.

Preview

For most Americans, the war of words that is raging so prominently in today's culture is smothering the very substance of what people are arguing about. Instead of seeking truth-based solutions to America's problems, people are usurping political control to silence all opposition. In a self-governed society such acrimony won't solve anything.

The following six questions are where today's war of words should be centered. If the Constitution is to be saved, the shouting must be replaced with civil dialogue about the most imperiled issue of our day: Liberty.

CHAPTER 1

Who will save the Constitution?

The Constitution itself cannot enforce its own virtues. It is the living administrators of the Constitution on whom this responsibility falls, those who make our government. If they uphold it, the Constitution's good form will open the way for good results. Whether or not they uphold it depends on the feelings and actions of the people who put such officers into positions of political power. [12]

The 3–4 Percent

Several observers point to the curious phenomenon that for any sizable group engaged in a task, typically only 3–4% will step forward to engage in the hard work, to serve as leaders, to serve as instructors, to do what others won't. All the other members tend to be followers or disengaged observers, waiting around to be told what to do. [13]

So will it be for America—a small minority of 3–4% of the population will step up to save the Constitution.

When the nation is on the verge of crumbling to pieces and tumbling to the ground, this 3–4% will trigger the nationwide resurgence that will snag the Constitution away from the brink of destruction.

First, they will instigate this reawakening by living in their own day-to-day lives the moral order and principles on which the Constitution is dependent; second, by upholding the Constitution in their local and state governments; and third, by learning enough about how self-government works to advise, guide, and help others to reengage with sound government.

A Million Levels of Influence

There will be some among the 3–4% with a broad circle of influence who will contribute to this salvation by sponsoring a needed amendment, by producing a daily radio or television program, by publishing a newspaper or web page, or by developing a multi-million dollar movie to educate the nation about the origins, foundation, and responsibilities necessary to sustain liberty.

At whatever level that minority of Americans find themselves, the burden of rescue falls to them—a cause to which they will be anxiously engaged for love of their families, love of their neighbors, and love of God.

These are the modern-day Founding Fathers, the modern-day Minutemen, the modern-day Continental Army, armed not with muskets and long rifles, but with knowledge, talent, wit, and their undying devotion to the principles of liberty.

Who are the 3–4 Percent?

Every person trying to save the Constitution is among the 3–4%. They won't be popular in their quest but they will stand on principle. They won't be extremists, but will represent all walks of life. They won't be exclusionary, but will invite everyone who desires liberty to join them. Those who draw public attention can expect to be mocked, scorned, exposed, humiliated, ridiculed, and rejected for their own human flaws.

As the ancient prophet Isaiah (750 B.C.) said of those trying to do good, enemies will come to silence and destroy them, to make them "an offender for a word, and lay a snare for him that reproveth in the gate, and turn aside the just for a thing of nought"[14]—but in the end, the 3-4% won't back down, they won't give up, and they won't abandon their convictions.

CHAPTER 2

What are we saving?

We want to save the original 1787 Constitution. We don't want to turn back the clock, but a restored Constitution will preserve the means whereby the clock may continue moving forward. The original Constitution, with a handful of logical and constitutionally legal corrections, embodies a brilliant framework of common-sense rules necessary for a nation to voluntarily govern itself.

Whenever we use the term "Constitution" we mean the original intent of the Framers when the Constitution was written; and to include the Bill of Rights; and, to include those additional amendments that did not weaken the people or expand the power of the federal government. Those nine benign amendments are numbers 11, 12, 13, 15, 19, 20, 21, 24, and 27.

Amendments that were injurious to the original intent of the Framers are numbers 14, 16, 17, 18, 22, 23, 25, and 26. A thorough examination of the controversies surrounding these eight amendments is important. However, that is not within the scope of this book. For a brief list of the major controversies connected to the eight injurious amendments, see *Endnotes.*[15]

James Madison said no government can be perfect, but "that which is least imperfect is therefore the best government."[16] The 1787 Constitution as correctly amended is the "least imperfect," and continues so to this very day. It is therefore the most preferred form of all.

Are there certain amendments that would correct some inadequacies and make it even more perfect? Yes, and those are summarized later. But the entire exercise of correcting imperfection is moot if the Constitution itself is destroyed.

CHAPTER 3

Who will save it?

T he Constitution will be restored when enough of the people really want it, and not before—that is the important challenge of our time.

Restoration will come after the American people undergo a humbling crisis of some form. It will probably be a series of events so disrupting and disturbing that the people will willingly turn from their innocent neglect—and for some, their deeply entrenched vanity, viciousness, rancor, hatred, and self-indulgence—and unitedly work to regain their religious and moral values. These are the same values that not many decades ago held secure America's traditional and prosperous culture.

This cycle of rise and fall in which America is now ensnared is as old as history—it's a long-established pattern where nations rise to power and prosperity, become prideful, start to ignore the roots of their strength, begin to indulge in corruptive behavior, and fall into decay and disarray.[17]

Ancient Israel cycled through that process many dozens of times. Nehemiah (445 B.C.) pointed out that every time the Israelites became powerful they would grow prideful and forget their roots. This led to corruption, neglect, and weakness. Then they'd be attacked. When the losses became severe, they'd become humble, pray for deliverance, and God would give them guidance and strength to become free. As they recovered and grew strong they'd become prideful—again—and throw away God's laws, kill the prophets, and being morally weak, be attacked. The fear and oppression would serve to humble them and open their hearts to the prophets. They would start obeying God's law and praying for deliverance. Salvation would come—again—and the process repeated itself over and over and over. Nehemiah concludes his historical summary saying "Nevertheless for [God's] great mercies' sake [he] didst not utterly consume them ..." (Nehemiah 9:31)

Henning Webb Prentis Jr. described this very cycle as a nation moving "From bondage to spiritual faith; from spiritual faith to courage; from courage to freedom; from freedom to abundance; from abundance to selfishness; from selfishness to complacency; from

Historical cycle of the rise and fall of nations

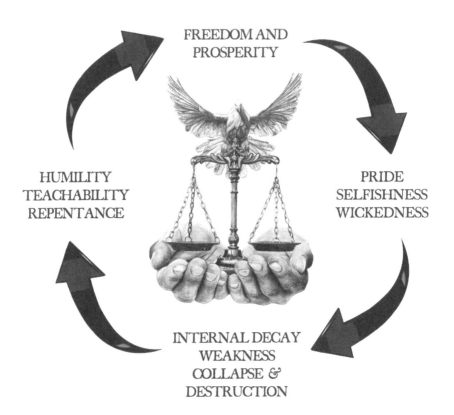

FREEDOM AND
PROSPERITY

PRIDE
SELFISHNESS
WICKEDNESS

HUMILITY
TEACHABILITY
REPENTANCE

INTERNAL DECAY
WEAKNESS
COLLAPSE &
DESTRUCTION

complacency to apathy; from apathy to fear; from fear to dependency; and from dependency back to bondage once more." [18]

Likewise, America will not be "utterly consumed." The conditions needed to save the Constitution will most likely await a similar cleansing of America's culture—probably instigated by internal decay as was the case for ancient Israel, Rome, Greece, China, India, Sumer, Inca, and dozens of other civilizations. [19]

Until that future day, a critically important window of opportunity is open for the 3–4% to lay a strong foundation on which correction and restoration may be built.

The authors' optimism for a restored Constitution rests on the patient principle of the oyster and the dreaded grain of sand. Once that particle of sand or a parasite enters the oyster's world it creates an irritation the unwilling host immediately labors to expel. If that fails, the oyster eases its discomfort by forming a sac around the particle, layering it with nacre, the same material used to line its shell, sometimes

Cycle of self-correction for nations framed in natural law

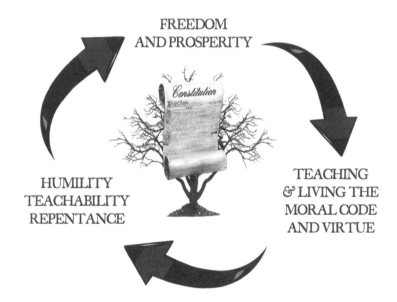

FREEDOM AND PROSPERITY

TEACHING & LIVING THE MORAL CODE AND VIRTUE

HUMILITY TEACHABILITY REPENTANCE

called mother of pearl. As the luminous substance hardens, and more layers are repeatedly formed around the particle, a pearl is formed.

Pearls take time. Saving the Constitution will take time.

By allowing this treatise and others like it to serve the role of the irritant, that amazing process of making our pearl can begin. There will develop within our lifetimes a beautiful pearl—a saved, restored, and strengthened Constitution.

In Matthew chapter 13, Jesus speaks of obtaining a beautiful pearl. "Again, the kingdom of heaven is like unto a merchant man, seeking goodly pearls: Who, when he had found one pearl of great price, went and sold all that he had, and bought it."[20]

Creating and obtaining the goodly pearl will take a period of patient endurance. And so must our labors mimic those of the merchant—to patiently invest all that we are able so that we may obtain a restored Constitution, our pearl of great price.

CHAPTER 4

Where will we save it?

"We are no longer fighting to defend a way of life—we are fighting to get it back."[21]

The "where" that the Constitution will be saved is first in the individual heart. The American people will need to begin living the virtues, values, and principles of self-government in their own personal lives and daily actions before they can expect to live them as a nation.

This monumental undertaking cannot be mobilized on a massive nationwide scale until enough people have privately prepared themselves for this fruitful challenge. The starting place for this transformation will be the leaders. Populations in general will follow the directions and standards established by their leadership. They do this more because of their lack of interest or typical inattentiveness than a strong desire for direct engagement. When the people become knowledgeable about correct principles and the workings of freedom they are more watchful over their leaders.

To live in a nation of political self-government the people must first commit to personal self-governance. That means wanting to live the moral principles of right and wrong, voluntarily and without force.[22] It is in that personally sacred vault of the individual human heart where the Constitution must undergo its truest ratification.

Today a large segment of society is experimenting with "anything goes" instead of exercising personal restraint and responsibility. The Framers warned repeatedly that experimenting with any theories short of the true principles of self-government would flounder and ultimately fail.

Each individual American will need to learn enough about the Constitution, its history and principles, so that the reasons for sustaining it on a personal basis are self evident. It requires learning more about it and its history, at home and school, asking questions and searching out the answers, learning to recognize true principles, and learning how the Constitution guides all activities toward prosperity.

When that standard of personal responsibility is adopted in the hearts of enough leaders and the nation as a whole, then civility in the national dialogue will return. It will be safe again to openly express opposing viewpoints. And then these additional steps to save the Constitution can be taken:

- Positive, pro-Constitution actions in Congress can be simultaneously invoked to shrink government, to re-establish the boundaries of power to where they were originally placed— the people will expect that.
- The courts could simultaneously start applying the original intent of the Constitution as a guideline to legal matters, to undo or redo, and no longer impose private interpretations according to individual, social, and political agendas—the people will expect that.
- The government could then return to serving the people instead of serving itself—the people will demand that.

CHAPTER 5

Why will we save it?

e want to save the Constitution to prevent the rise of another monarchy of elitists—a king—the very antithesis of individual freedom.

The American success formula allowed a small segment of the human family, less than six percent, to become the richest industrial nation on earth. It allowed them to originate more than half of the world's total production and enjoy the highest standard of living in the history of the world.

It also produced a very generous people. No nation in all the recorded annals of history has shared so much of its wealth with every other nation as has the United States of America. Even when it loaned money, it often forgave the debt.

The American Founding Fathers were students and philosophers as well as soldiers and politicians. They carefully scrutinized every system of government in existence to see which one was the most likely to enable humanity to attain freedom, prosperity, and peace. But among all the political systems of the day, there was no such government. Every government around the globe was structured to exploit its people, reduce them to poverty, and marshal their intimidated youth into predatory wars against nearby nations. "Is there at this moment," asked Charles Pinckney of South Carolina in 1788, "a nation upon earth that enjoys this right, where the true principles of representation are understood and practiced, and where all authority flows from and returns at stated periods to the people? I answer, there is not."[23]

All existing governments, he said, owed their births to "fraud, to force, or accident."[24]

The Greatest Achievement.

The "why" Americans must save the Constitution is to keep the political powers separated: The legislative, executive, and judiciary branches separated from each other and from the states—all confined within their own well-defined boundaries. This is the single most important and empowering achievement that came out of the Constitutional Convention.

Combining those powers into a single person, group, or branch of government is precisely how liberty is destroyed. Said James Madison in 1788, "The accumulation of all powers, legislative, executive, and judiciary, in the same hands, whether of one, a few, or many, may justly be pronounced the very definition of tyranny."[25]

Jefferson saw the seeds of tyranny years before the Constitution was born. He warned in 1784, "An elective despotism was not the government we fought for; but one ... in which the powers of government should be so divided and balanced among several bodies of magistracy, as that no one could transcend their legal limits."[26] He warned that the collapse of separation would be the courts' doing: "The engine of consolidation will be the federal judiciary; the two other branches, the corrupting and corrupted instruments."[27]

We want to save the Constitution to maintain the distinct, clean, and well-defined separation of political powers. Without that, our ending is certain: The nation will slip into an abyss of modern slavery, ruled over by an elitist American monarchy of 10,000 crowns.

CHAPTER 6

How will we save it?

T he "how" component to save the Constitution is fraught with chaos. It runs completely wild among the people for lack of a common starting place, a shared perspective, a unified set of goals, and a basic set of knowledge and facts. There are also the broad differences in individual skills, determination, and resources. Those variables throw confusion into the important process of how we go about saving the Constitution. But that's not all.

Single-issue Warriors.

Many Americans focus on just a small number of specific issues they find most important, but at the same time remain relatively aloof to the demands of other claimants.

Ignorance.

Surprisingly, most Americans who want to save the Constitution have never read it. Many of those who have read it didn't ask the right questions so they could see the answers the Framers provided. For them the Constitution's relevancy to freedom and current events is lost even though they sense its enormous importance.

Impatience.

Anxious Americans want the best answer delivered to them right now. This drive to excel, the byproduct of the freedom to innovate and express, leaves little time to study the issues in-depth, and many Americans prefer quick solutions they can rally behind and support. This may be a natural human trait and something to be expected in today's super-accelerated world, but impatience to become self-educated about liberty remains nevertheless one of the most difficult hurdles to overcome.

Doomsayers.

Hundreds of books already address what's wrong with America. They inform but they're also a discouraging read, lacking hope and a way forward. A part of the population has turned from these energy-draining prophets of gloom, and are shrinking away into hopeless apathy. They're starving for hope and direction.

Technicians.

Many Americans pin their hopes on one-dimensional solutions such as new amendments and statutes to solve our national issues: *If we could just repeal the 16th and 17th amendments, pass a Judiciary Reform Amendment, clarify the Commerce Clause, the Welfare Clause, and impose a Balanced Budget Amendment, then the lion's share of America's problems would be cured.* These technical fixes are necessary repairs but they are risky assumptions in today's corrupted culture. They presuppose that once such amendments are ratified, the people and the government will faithfully obey them as intended.

Progressives.

People who believe the Constitution is an evolving idea that was meant to change with the times see no reason to save its original form. They hope for a strong central government to control and change the people by force. These Americans neglect to address the most important component of self-government that lies at the root of everything: Human nature.

Human nature does not evolve. It does not change with new technology, new economics, or new philosophies. It is ever-present and constant. Progressives' biggest blunder is failing to see how the Constitution balances the proclivities of human nature with the proper management of political power. They don't seem to understand how that balanced restraint prevents a monarchy of elitists from taking control—unless that's exactly what they want: To collapse society and use the resulting chaos and anarchy as a means to install themselves as holders of all political power.

Progressives unknowingly doom themselves to repeat the fatal failures of antiquity by pretending that a broken Constitution is a better Constitution.

Fake Values.

Eliminating common Bible-based values has burned ugly, blood-soaked holes in the fabric of American society, leaving the general population in great confusion. At every level people are wandering to and fro through the cultural landscape wondering what values they may claim in the face of conflicting views, of ugly bigotry and faith shaming, of rejection of traditional values, and of unpopular allegiances.

The rising generation has lost its ability to think for itself. It is being deluded into believing that traditional values are oppressive, unfair, impolite, racist, or demeaning. The prophet Isaiah (750 B.C.) succinctly framed America's biggest problem of today:

"Woe unto them that call evil good, and good evil; that put darkness for light, and light for darkness; that put bitter for sweet, and sweet for bitter!" (Isaiah 5:20)

In other words, as Albert Bowen said, "That which is right does not become wrong merely because it may be deserted by the majority, neither does that which is wrong today become right tomorrow by the chance circumstance that it has won the approval or been adopted by overwhelmingly predominant numbers. Principles cannot be changed by nor accommodate themselves to the vagaries of popular sentiment."[28]

The devastating fallout from today's "good is evil" culture is tens of millions of youth turning to social media and radicalized trend setters to define their moral values. A culture of "anything goes" is replacing the culture of being self-sufficient, respectful of others, and other-oriented. That is, living the Golden Rule: Do unto others as you would have them do unto you.

The Anti-Constitutionals.

The loudest voices in recent times are from those who wish to kill the Constitution by a thousand cuts—not because of its perceived weaknesses, but because of its enormous strengths.

For more than a dozen decades the anti-Constitutionals have tried to sell alternative ideas as superior to virtue-based constitutional liberty. These ideas have come cloaked in such names as "the model of a new Constitution," "the second Bill of Rights," the progressive movement, socialism, democratic socialism, "A Square Deal All Around," the "New Deal," the "Great Society," "Putting People First," "Fundamentally Change America," "Green New Deal," "shared prosperity," "diversity," political correctness, communism, Nazism, theocracies, collectivism, totalitarianism, and dozens of others. Regardless of their titles, monikers, or philosophies, they are, in the end, all the same—they seek to eliminate private property ownership, disrupt the culture, undermine the institutions that stabilize the people, and ultimately remove power from the people to allow government force to control and change the people, to violate human rights, and to install all-powerful rulers. None of these old, tired forms can take root in America so long as the Constitution and national virtue are present to block the way.

Those calling for replacing the Constitution are not calling for something better—they are calling for more political power, with their own ideologies and people in charge of the rest of us.

The Reset.

America will not long endure the stresses put upon its people by the anti-Constitutionals and progressives and their pretended values. The ending place for these corruptions is easily predicted. Portions of the country will adhere to the traditional moral codes and principles upon which a civil society and the Constitution were built, and others will not.

As prosperity rises among the traditional cities and states, the dark depressions of impoverishment, elitism, class warfare, gangs, crime, envy, jealousy, deceit, self-serving leadership, and decay will visit the others. The traditional states will resort to temporary extremes: To protect themselves from spillover they'll increase state border security; they will actively teach and promote true values and moral codes at all levels of education and institutions of society; they will respect human rights but no longer kowtow to extremists and their demands to accept corrupted human behavior as a plausible alternative reality; they will resist outside influences that spread discord and corrupt the youth; and they will slam the door on evil addictions that are wreaking havoc among the peaceful.

Teach and Exemplify.

Somewhere in that process of regional upheaval, good Americans will wake up and reject the progressive movement's frontal attacks on Biblical morals, personal responsibilities, and traditional American values—and will look for the better way. The rest of America must be ready to teach and help them return to these values. It will be a reset of historic proportions, and a massive spike on the learning curve for many millions of citizens.

Preparations.

The manner whereby the Constitution will be reestablished will not make sense to those not familiar with how freedom works. In the next section, *The Founding Fathers' Book of Instructions* provides a succinct overview of the basic principles of liberty. These are the fundamentals that every American eventually will need to understand. There are no shortcuts to this end. The Constitution cannot be saved in ignorance.

Review Questions

1. Some have said a book claiming to explain "How to Save the Constitution" is impossible to write. If you sat down to create such a book, how would you begin? What would you list as the most important first steps to save the Constitution?

2. Do you consider yourself among the 3-4%? Why or why not?

3. When you read the Prophet Nehemiah's summary of ancient Israel, what thoughts did you have about the current state of America? Which of the two historical cycles illustrated on those pages do you believe America is now on, and at what part of that cycle does it stand today?

4. Do you think a "righteous government" is capable of making the American people a better people? Explain.

5. What are some modern examples of Isaiah's ancient prediction that in our day there would be wicked people daring to call evil good, good evil, and putting darkness for light, and light for darkness, and putting bitter for sweet and sweet for bitter?

LEARN THE BASIC PRINCIPLES OF LIBERTY

Learn People's Law.

Learn the reasons for a strong local government.

Learn the Framers' 28 great ideas that changed the world.

Preview

We can't save what we don't understand. We can't defend what we don't know. We can't teach what we haven't read.

The following pages are perhaps the most important of the entire text. It is upon these unchanging principles that all good government stands.

We can't save, defend, or teach liberty from a position of patriotic ignorance. To establish a position of patriotic authority, Americans must understand the basic principles of self-government well enough to teach them to others.

CHAPTER 7

People's Law

G overnment is a system of ruling or controlling. Most people see government as a political party such as democrat, republican, socialist, independent, labor party, etc. However, those names don't tell us very much about their plans for "ruling or controlling." That's why the American Framers measured the world's political systems according to how much power and political force they exercised over their people.

In other words, their measuring stick was not political parties but political power.

Using political power as the measuring stick, the Framers discovered that almost all political systems throughout history fall into one of two extremes: anarchy or tyranny.

The Problem of Anarchy and Tyranny

Anarchy is chaos. It's a system where there is no law, no government, no control, and no central political power. Those systems allow mobs to form and impose their will on others, and to take as they please. Stealing and fighting is normal, and there is no safety for anyone. In anarchy the biggest gang always wins.

Tyranny is at the opposite extreme. It is too much concentrated power, too much control, and too much government. Whatever the ruler commands, the people are forced to obey. That system is ancient and commonplace. It is usually called *Ruler's Law,* where the ruler makes all the laws and the ruler always wins.

Finding the Balanced Center

The Framers' goal was to find the right balance between too much political power and none at all.

Their solution is found in the Constitution where the people hold all of the controlling power. They may delegate and assign certain powers to the government, but always under the watchful care of their representatives. This system is rare and difficult to establish. It is usually called *People's Law.*

The Framers' view of these three forms of law and government might look like this:

All Power in the People

The difference between Ruler's Law and People's Law is illustrated with two pyramids.

In Ruler's Law all the power is held by the ruler at the top level as shown by the inverted pyramid. The lower units of government are granted fewer powers until, at the bottom layer, the individual is granted the least power of all.

In People's Law all the power is in the people as shown at the base of the upright pyramid. The higher units of government are granted fewer powers up to the highest level, the national government, which has the least power of all. The orientation of the pyramids illustrates that Ruler's Law is vulnerable to toppling, while People's Law is more stable and harder to disturb. [29]

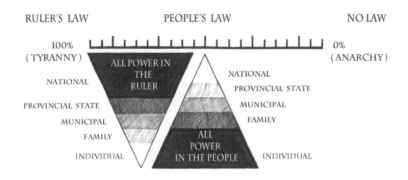

Balancing Power at the Top Levels of Government

One of the biggest debates at the Constitutional Convention was how to be unified as a nation but avoid the tyranny of another overbearing, overly powerful central government.

The Framers were acutely aware of this danger, so they carried this concept of a balanced center a step further. They designed the Constitution to maintain political balance between the states on the one side, and the federal government on the other. The states carried the greater load of power so they could deal with the internal workings of the country. The federal government's responsibility was to handle issues too big for just one state, such as international affairs that required a unified voice and presence from the United States of America. The states agreed to this balance, but with a built-in degree of distrust and jealousy.

Left Wing, Right Wing

This balanced structure also created two positive forces for helping the nation grow and prosper. This is illustrated with an American Eagle swooping across the landscape with both wings fully deployed.

Wing #1, its left wing, is the problem-solving wing. Those who focus on problems are sensitive to the unfulfilled needs of the people. They dream of various plans to make corrections.

Wing #2, its right wing, has the responsibility of conserving the nation's resources and the people's freedom. Its function is to analyze the programs of wing #1 with two questions. First, can we afford it? Secondly, what will it do to the rights and individual freedoms of the people?

Both Wings Are Essential

If both wings fulfill their assigned function, the American eagle will fly straighter and higher than any civilization in the history of the world. But if either of these wings goes to sleep on the job, the American eagle will drift toward anarchy or tyranny.

For example, if wing #1, the problem-solving side, becomes infatuated with the idea of solving all the problems of the nation regardless of the cost, and wing #2 fails to sober up the problem solvers with a more realistic approach, the eagle will spin off toward the left, which is tyranny.

On the other hand, if wing #1 fails to see the problems which need solving and wing #2 becomes inflexible in its course of not solving problems simply to save money, or to avoid disturbing the status quo, then government loses its credibility and the eagle drifts over toward the right where the people decide to take matters into their own hands. This can disintegrate into anarchy.

The Three-headed Eagle

LEGISLATIVE
House   Senate
EXECUTIVE   **JUDICIAL**

#1
The Problem-Solving
Wing

#2
The Conservation
Wing

The Framers' distribution of political power can be illustrated as a three-headed eagle. The central head, the Legislature, watches with two eyes—the House and the Senate. All three heads share the same neck, meaning there is both separation of powers but they must coordinate to get their work done. None may act independently of the others. This relationship could be called "coordination without consolidation."

CHAPTER 8

Strong Local Self-government Guards Against Corruption

Saving the Constitution as a goal has stalled because many patriots don't understand the simple basics of setting up a free society. The central ingredient is the separation of powers. That means distributing government authority to that level where a particular function is best handled.

The states became the key structures for managing the people on the most intimate levels of community life. The Framers designed it that way to keep the people in control and in charge—and to keep the federal government far removed from state business. It all begins with the rights of the individual.

The Individual

The Founders perceived "the people" as individuals with the unalienable right to exercise their free agency in governing their own affairs so long as they did no harm to the rights of others. They felt the individual has both the right and the responsibility to solve most of the problems relating to work, play, associations, creature comforts, education, acquisition and disposition of property, and the effort needed to make a person self-sustaining. As a member of society, the individual has a right to vote. He or she has an inherent right to enjoy all of the general privileges and prerogatives enjoyed by the other members of society.

The Family

On the second level is the family which the Founders considered to be the most important unit of organized society. It is within the family circle that individuals tend to find greater satisfaction and self-realization than in any other segment of the community, state, or nation. The family is granted exclusive and sovereign rights which cannot be invaded by any other branch of government unless:

1. There is evidence of extended and extreme neglect of children.
2. There is evidence of criminal abuse.
3. The family residence is being used for criminal purposes.

At the same time the family has inescapable responsibilities. Parents are responsible for the conduct of their children, the education of their children, the religious training of their children, and the responsibility of raising children to be morally competent, self-sustaining adults.

Social workers and state officials may not agree with the religious training, choice of schools, philosophy of child-rearing, or other details in the life of a family, but the doctrine of *parens patriae* (the right of the state to intervene) does not arise unless one or more of the above criminal or abuse situations is present.

The Community

There are a number of things which a community of families can do better than an individual family. This is the basis for the incorporated community. It has the responsibility to provide roads, schools, water, police protection, city courts to handle misdemeanors, etc. It also has the power to tax for the purpose of providing these specific services.

The County

There are a number of activities which a group of communities can handle collectively with more efficiency than as individual communities. These include the prosecution of serious crimes or minor crimes in the rural area, the providing of a secure long-term county jail (for prisoners serving less than a year); providing county roads, bridges, and drainage systems; providing rural schools, and rural police services; levying and collecting taxes based on the assessed value of property; issuing licenses for fishing and hunting as well as marriages; keeping records of deeds, births, deaths, and marriages; conducting elections, caring for the needy, and protecting public health.

The State

The state is the sovereign entity of a specified region which can function more effectively for all of the communities, counties, and people of the state than they could do for themselves. The state has the authority to tax, facilitate commerce, establish courts, define crime and prescribe punishment, establish and maintain public schools, build roads and bridges, and supervise intrastate waterways. The state can also pass laws to protect the health, safety, and morals of its people. Moral problems include such matters as alcohol, illegal gambling, misuse of certain dangerous drugs, prostitution, and other culture-collapsing behaviors.

Private Morality and Public Morality

An important social barrier regarding corrupt morals and the rest of society is that the state can only intervene in issues where public morality is involved. Private morality is a matter between a person and his conscience. He has the private moral right to do anything he pleases so long as he does no harm to others. However, the moment his moral behavior violates the quality of life of the majority of the community, that person is in the arena of public morality and must abide by the will of the majority. In his *Commentaries* (1765), Sir William Blackstone described the distinction between private and public morals. He said:

"No matter how abandoned may be a man's principles, or how vicious his practice, provided he keeps his wickedness to himself, and does not violate public decency, he is out of the reach of human laws. But if he makes his vices public, then they become by his bad example, of pernicious [destructive] effect to society, and it is the business of human laws to correct them."[30]

The Founders set up the states so they were a projection of the will of the people, not an auxiliary branch of the national government. In the states' area of assigned responsibilities, their power was plenary (absolute), sovereign, and exclusive. In a very narrow area there was joint responsibility with the federal government.

And within the states was meant to dwell a great check on the federal government's powers. As Jefferson said, "What country can preserve its liberties, if its rulers are not warned from time to time, that this people preserve the spirit of resistance?"[31]

The Principles

Next, *The Founding Fathers' Book of Instructions* gives a brief overview of the universal ideas underpinning self-government. Knowing these principles builds the framework whereby people can more quickly detect the violation of natural laws, so they can take corrective action.

CHAPTER 9

People's Law is Grounded on 28 Principles

T here was hardly a single idea that the American Founding Fathers put into their formula that someone hadn't thought of before. Even so, by the time the Constitution was being written in 1787, none of those ideas was being substantially practiced anywhere in the world. It was in America that the Framers assembled the 28 great ideas that produced the dynamic success formula which proved such a sensational blessing to modern man.

These basic principles are found repeatedly talked about among the Framers' writings, and make up what they later described as their "indispensable" road map to attain America's divine or "manifest destiny."

Principle 1. The only basis for sound government is Natural Law.

Natural law is God's law, and it governs the entire universe. On its most basic level Natural Law is seen operating as the laws of chemistry, physics and biology. On the higher level it is seen maintaining moral respect among the people. When the people protect natural law and unalienable rights for one another, they prosper. Thomas Jefferson called these laws "the laws of nature and of nature's God."[32]

Principle 2. A free people cannot survive under a republican constitution unless they remain virtuous and morally strong.

Only a virtuous people may live in self-government. Professor Gordon S. Wood examined how the Founding Generation viewed the concept of virtue: "[Each person] must somehow be persuaded to submerge his personal wants into the greater good of the whole. This willingness of the individual to sacrifice his private interest for the good of the community—such patriotism or love of country—the eighteenth century mind termed public virtue ... A popularly based government cannot be supported without virtue."[33]

When there is a breakdown of religious faithfulness, there inescapably follows deterioration in the political morality.[34] George Washington promised, "The general government ... can never be in danger of degenerating into a monarchy, an oligarchy, an aristocracy, or any other despotic or oppressive form, so long as there shall remain any virtue in the body of the people."[35]

Principle 3. The most promising method of securing a virtuous people is to elect virtuous leaders.

Leaders have a sacred responsibility to point the way to excellence in all things. But leaders also reflect the goodness or badness of the people from whom they emerge. Samuel Adams observed that "Neither the wisest constitution nor the wisest laws will secure the liberty and happiness of a people whose manners are universally corrupt. He therefore is the truest friend to the liberty of his country who tries most to promote its virtue, and who ... will not suffer a man to be chosen into any office of power and trust who is not a wise and virtuous man."[36]

Principle 4. Without religion the government of a free people cannot be maintained.

The importance of religion in self-government was a major theme of the Framers. They emphasized the Bible rather than individual creeds. For example, when the Northwest Ordinance was passed by Congress in 1787, it encouraged "religion, morality and knowledge" to be taught in the schools. No religious creed was specified, but Biblical religion is implied.

Thomas Jefferson said these basic beliefs are the principles "in which God has united us all."[37] John Adams called these the "general principles" on which the American civilization had been founded.[38] Samuel Adams said these basic beliefs constituted "the religion of America," which is also "the religion of all mankind."[39] George Washington said religion and morality are "indispensable supports" of self-government.[40] Indispensable means absolutely necessary.

Principle 5. All things were created by God, therefore upon him all mankind are equally dependent, and to him they are equally responsible.

Being unified on the same set of moral codes and principles is the only foundation on which self-government can stand. In John Locke's *Essay Concerning Human Understanding*, the Framers found clarity about the Creator and his role in revealing the requirements for successful self-government. They considered the existence of the Creator as the most fundamental premise underlying *all* self-evident truth. The Creator would have a sense of right and wrong and feel indignation or anger when "right conduct" is violated. Since mankind were made in the "image of God" people can know the Creator is intelligent, has a sense of humor, and a sense of beauty, and that he has organized everything according to fantastic qualities of form, color, and contrasts.

Principle 6. All mankind were created equal.

No two human beings were created exactly alike in any respect. Each one is born with different looks, different tastes, different skills. They are different in physical strength, mental capacity, emotional stability; in their inherited social and economic status; in their opportunities for self-fulfillment, and scores of other ways. Being "created equal"stands only in these three ways: Equal before God; equal before the law; and equal in the protection of their rights. The highest goal in self-government is to see that these principles of equality become a reality.

Principle 7. The proper role of government is to protect equal rights, not provide equal things.

The Founders recognized that the people cannot delegate to their government any power except that which they have the lawful right to exercise themselves. For example, every person is entitled to the protection of life, liberty, and property. Therefore it is perfectly legitimate to set up a police force to protect these unalienable rights. But an individual has no right to take personal property from a neighbor just because he doesn't have something. And likewise, the government has no inherent right to take property from the "have's" just to dole it out to the "have-nots."

Principle 8. Mankind are endowed by God with certain unalienable rights.

A "right" is a legal or ethical entitlement. There are two basic rights— those granted by the government, and those we are born with called unalienable rights. Our unalienable rights are universal and established by the Creator. Examples include life, liberty, and the pursuit of happiness; and, the right to choose, acquire, and develop property, to associate with anyone, to self-defense, to compassion, to try, buy, sell, and fail. Laws protecting the family and the institution of marriage are all based on God's law. All of these are unalienable rights. The struggle for freedom is the struggle to exercise unalienable rights.[41]

Principle 9. To protect human rights, God has revealed a code of divine law.

The Bible contains the principles and moral code needed for self-government. The revered English jurist Sir William Blackstone (1723–1780) observed that the Creator is a being of infinite wisdom, and has laid down laws of right and wrong that are eternal and unchangeable. And, he enabled "human reason to discover, so far as they are necessary for the conduct of human actions ... that we should live honestly, should hurt nobody, and should render to everyone his due."[42] Blackstone said these revealed laws are "found only in the Holy Scriptures," and are an original part of Natural Law because "they tend in all their consequences to man's felicity."[43] In other words, obedience to Natural Law, the divine law, brings true peace and joy.

Principle 10. The God-given right to govern is vested in the sovereign authority of the whole people.

People are not born to be slaves to an emperor or monarch. They have the right to assemble and establish their own government. The English politician Algernon Sidney (1623–1683) stood up publicly against King Charles II to declare that same truth. The king was horrified and had him beheaded. This helped trigger a revolution that overthrew the king in 1688, putting Parliament in charge over the monarchy. A century later, the Framers wove this principle directly into every aspect of the Constitution. Said James Madison, "the ultimate authority ... resides in the people alone."[44]

Principle 11. The majority of the people may alter or abolish a government which has become tyrannical.

The Founders were well acquainted with the vexations resulting from an abusive, tyrannical government. Thomas Jefferson said that if any people suffers from such despotism "it is their right, it is their duty, to throw off such government, and to provide new guards for their future security."[45]

However, John Locke emphasized that there is no right of revolt against the government by individuals or a minority. They must seek their remedy in the courts. It is only when a clear majority of the people have been seriously abused—so that there is a united spirit of determined action by practically the whole people—that rebellion against the government has any chance of success.[46]

Principle 12. The United States of America shall be a republic.

Theoretically, a democracy requires the full participation of all the people to pass laws or in the decision-making procedures of the government. It means "one man, one vote."

This has never worked because the people always become so occupied with their daily tasks that they will not properly study the issues nor will they take the time to test the merits of the issues under consideration. They become vulnerable to making emotional decisions instead of studious and fact-based decisions.

The American Founders wanted to use the democratic method of mass participation in electing representatives, but after the election they wanted to be governed by these representatives. And that is what "republican" means—government by elected representatives.

Principle 13. A Constitution should protect the people from the frailties of their rulers.

The genius of the Constitution is that it was specifically designed to keep government in the balanced center. It was given enough power to maintain order and justice but not enough power to abuse the people. This was achieved by a Constitutional separation of powers among the three branches of government. Each branch has power to check the powers of the other two.

Also, there is a specific list of 20 powers (see Article I, Section 8)[47] delegated to the federal government. And the Tenth Amendment makes it unconstitutional for any branch of government to try to exercise additional powers.

Principle 14. Life and liberty are secure only so long as the rights of property are secure.

The three foremost unalienable rights mentioned in the first constitution of Massachusetts were "Life, Liberty and Property." Property has no rights, but a person does—the right to acquire, develop, and dispose of property. The government's primary purpose is to preserve that right from abuse by both the government and fellow citizens. The Founders warned against letting the government take from the "have's" and give to the "have-not's," even for positive projects. The generosity of the community holding *problems* in common instead of trying to have *things* in common has always done a better job. As President Grover Cleveland said, "The friendliness and charity of our countrymen can always be relied upon to relieve their fellow-citizens in misfortune."[48]

Principle 15. The highest level of prosperity occurs when there is a free-market economy and a minimum of government regulations.

The United States was the first country to build its whole national economy on natural law. These principles were brought to light by Adam Smith in 1776 in his five books called *The Wealth of Nations.* His natural-law formula for free economics called for the freedom to try, the freedom to buy, the freedom to sell, and the freedom to fail.

However, a successful economy must depend upon the government to prevent four corrosive elements:

1. The use of illegal *force* in the marketplace to compel buyers or sellers to violate their free will.

2. The use of *fraud* in misrepresenting the quality, location or ownership of items being bought and sold.

3. The greedy exploitation of *monopoly.* This eliminates competition and results in the restraint of trade.

4. *Debauchery* of the moral fiber of society by commercial exploitation of vice, pornography, obscenity, drugs, liquor, prostitution, or gambling.

Principle 16. The government should be separated into three branches.

This brilliant idea of three separate but united branches dates back to Polybius, a Greek who lived 204–122 B.C. His ideas laid dormant until the mid-1770s when Baron Charles de Montesquieu brought them to the ongoing debates about good government. He said there should be a single executive, a legislature of two houses—a lower house to be the elected representatives of the people, and the upper house to represent the states. He also felt there should be an independent judiciary to see that the other departments of government did not violate their constitutional parameters. John Adams was the first American statesman to begin promoting the ideas of Montesquieu, and was successful in getting his ideas incorporated into the U.S. Constitution. It was a difference that made *all* the difference.

Principle 17. A system of checks and balances should be adopted to prevent the abuse of power by the different branches of government.

James Madison had to spend five issues of the Federalist Papers (47 to 51) to explain the genius of the separation of powers and then turn around and explain why they all had to be carefully laced back together to provide the necessary checks and balances so that no department of government could become abusive. As it turned out, the Framers achieved a system of checks and balances far more refined and complex than Montesquieu ever envisioned.

Principle 18. The unalienable rights of the people are most likely to be preserved if the principles of government are set forth in a written Constitution.

A written Constitution is more immune to arbitrary change than an oral or traditional constitution. England still does not have a written constitution and therefore the latest act of Parliament is enforced as part of its constitutional structure. The structure of the American system is set forth in the Constitution of the United States and the only weaknesses which have appeared are those which were allowed to creep in despite the written words of the Constitution.

Principle 19. Only limited and carefully defined powers should be delegated to government, all others being retained by the people.

One of the reasons many of the states would not adopt the original draft of the Constitution was because there was no specific bill of rights. The first ten amendments were therefore added to include the ancient unalienable rights long abused by dictators.

The Ninth Amendment is the catch-all provision:

"The enumeration in the Constitution of certain rights shall not be construed to deny or disparage *others* retained by the people."

The Tenth Amendment is the most widely violated provision of the bill of rights. If it had been respected and enforced America would be an amazingly different country than it is today. This amendment provides:

"The powers not delegated to the United States by the Constitution, nor prohibited by it to the States, are reserved to the States respectively, or to the people."

Principle 20. The government must operate according to the will of the majority, but Constitutional provisions must be made to protect the rights of the minority.

The Framers found in John Locke's writings an excellent discussion on majority rule and minority rights. He wrote that when a person chooses to join others in a great confederation of groups and peoples, he is also bound to "submit to the determination of the majority."[49] Locke pointed out that governing on any other basis, such as requiring 100 percent consensus on every issue brought forward, simply can't work because there would always be, on *every* vote, a dissenter who would prevent a 100 percent vote. Locke said that is "next [to] impossible ever to be had."[50]

Accepting majority rule as a practical necessity puts the minority at risk unless their basic rights are protected in spite of the majority. Protecting minority rights is what the Constitution and the Bill of Rights were designed to do. While not yet perfect, considerable progress toward protecting minority rights has been made.

Principle 21. Strong local self-government is the keystone to preserving human freedom.

Thomas Jefferson said the best way to a good and safe government is not to concentrate it all in one, but "to divide it among the many, distributing to every one exactly the functions he is competent [to perform best]." He said to leave the issues best handled by a national government to that level, such as national defense and federal relations, but leave the states "with the civil rights, laws, police and administration of what concerns the State generally; the counties with the local concerns of the counties, and each ward [township] direct the interests within itself."[51]

Principle 22. A free people should be governed by law and not by the whims of men.

The Founders believed that where there is no law there can be no freedom. As John Locke said, "The end of law is not to abolish or restrain, but to preserve and enlarge freedom. For in all the states of created beings, capable of laws, where there is no law there is no freedom."[52]

The other side of that issue is the need that the law is stationary, fixed, and permanent. If every new political party in power changed the laws, there would be a constant state of chaos. James Madison said if the law may "undergo such incessant changes that no man, who knows what the law is today, can guess what it will be tomorrow" would be in a state of constant violation and confusion. He said "Law is defined to be a rule of action, but how can that be a rule which is little known and less fixed."[53]

Principle 23. A free society cannot survive as a republic without a broad program of general education.

Knowledge is power, and knowledge is freedom. Being ignorant of personal rights and the authority of those with political power is enslavement by ignorance. John Adams stated, that from the earliest colonial days, Americans considered education the main-sail for freedom and human progress: "Liberty cannot be preserved without a general knowledge among the people ... They have a right, an indisputable unalienable, indefeasible, divine right to the most dreaded kind of knowledge—I mean, of the character and conduct of their rulers."[54]

Principle 24. A free people will not survive unless they stay strong.

It was the philosophy of the Founders that the kind hand of providence had been everywhere present in allowing the United States to come forth as the first free people in modern times. They further felt they would forever be blessed with freedom and prosperity if they remained virtuous and well-armed. Trusting to the mercy and benevolence of an enemy was deemed foolishness of the most severe degree. Benjamin Franklin said "Our security lies, I think, in our growing strength, both in numbers and wealth ... for there is much truth in the Italian saying, 'Make yourselves sheep, and the wolves will eat you.'" [55]

Washington's position on national defense was in terms of grim realities experienced on the field of battle. There is no question, he said, that "To be prepared for war is one of the most effectual means of preserving peace." [56]

Principle 25. "Peace, commerce, and honest friendship with all nations—entangling alliances with none."

These are the words of Thomas Jefferson, given in his first inaugural address. [57] This was the Founders' original doctrine of "separatism." It was far different from the modern term of "isolationism." Isolationism implies a complete seclusion from other nations, as though the United States were to be detached and somehow incubated in isolation from other nations. North Korea is isolationist, Switzerland is separatist. The Founders wanted to be Switzerland.

George Washington said: "The great rule of conduct for us, in regard to foreign nations, is in extending our commercial relations to have as little political connection as possible." [58]

Principle 26. The core unit which determines the strength of any society is the family; therefore the government should foster and protect its integrity.

The family is the great stabilizer of society. There is nothing new to this important principle; it's as ancient as human history. From a strong marriage comes a strong family. Said the Apostle Paul, "Neither is the man without the woman, neither the woman without the man, in the Lord."[59]

Benjamin Franklin said marriage is "the most natural state of man, and therefore the state in which you are most likely to find solid happiness. ...It is the man and woman united that make the complete human being ...Together they are more likely to succeed in the world."[60]

About raising children John Locke said "The power, then, that parents have over their children arises from that duty which is incumbent on them, to take care of their offspring during the imperfect state of childhood. To inform the mind, and govern the actions of their yet ignorant [youth], till reason shall take its place and ease them of that trouble, is what the children want, and the parents are bound to [provide]. ...When he has acquired that state [of maturity], he is presumed to know how far that law is to be his guide, and how far he may make use of his freedom."[61]

And from that intimate guidance are law-abiding citizens raised to sustain, support, and participate in the orderly process of creativity and industry in a land of liberty.

Alexis de Tocqueville noted that peace in America is a consequence of peace in the home: "There is certainly no country in the world where the tie of marriage is more respected than in America, or where conjugal happiness is more highly or worthily appreciated. In Europe almost all the disturbances of society arise from the irregularities of domestic life."[62]

Principle 27. The burden of debt is as destructive to human freedom as subjugation by conquest.

The Founders knew that borrowing can be an honorable procedure in a time of emergency, but they deplored it just the same. They looked upon debt as a temporary handicap which should be paid off at the earliest possible moment.

The Founders knew that excessive debt greatly curtails the freedom of the debtor. It also obscures his search for happiness. There is the sense of waste—much like the man who has to make payments on a dead horse. Where the national debt was made necessary by an emergency such as a war, Jefferson said "We are bound to defray expenses [of the war] within our own time, and are unauthorized to burden posterity with them ... We shall all consider ourselves morally bound to pay them ourselves and consequently within the life [expectancy] of the majority."[63]

Principle 28. The United States has a manifest destiny to eventually become a glorious example of God's law under a restored Constitution that will inspire the entire human race.

The Founders sensed from the very beginning that they were on a divine mission. Their great disappointment was that it didn't all come to pass in their day. John Adams wrote "I always consider the settlement of America with reverence and wonder, as the opening of a grand scene and design in Providence for the illumination of the ignorant, and the emancipation of the slavish part of mankind all over the earth."[64]

Thomas Jefferson looked upon the development of freedom under the Constitution as "the world's best hope," and in 1801 he wrote that what had been accomplished in the United States by 1801 would be "a standing monument and example for the aim and imitation of people of other countries."[65]

When the Constitution was being ratified, Alexander Hamilton noted, "It has been frequently remarked that it seems to have been reserved to the people of this country, by their conduct and example, to decide the important question whether societies of men are really capable or not of establishing good government from reflection and choice or whether they are forever destined to depend for their political constitutions on accident and force."[66]

James Madison summed up the feelings of the Founders when he said:

"Had no important step been taken by the leaders of the Revolution for which a precedent could not be discovered, no government established of which an exact model did not present itself, the people of the United States might at this moment have been numbered among the melancholy victims of misguided councils, must at best have been laboring under the weight of some of those forms which have crushed the liberties of the rest of mankind."

Then he continued:

"Happily for America, happily we trust *for the whole human race*, they pursued a new and more noble course. They accomplished a revolution which had no parallel in the annals of human society. They reared the fabrics of governments which have no model on the face of the globe. They formed the design of a great Confederacy, which it is incumbent on their successors to *improve and perpetuate.*"[67]

Therein lies the challenge to modern Americans. At some point we are obligated by divine injunction to "improve and perpetuate" what the Founding Fathers began.

CHAPTER 10

The Four Pillars of People's Law

he 28 principles are the great ideas that changed the world. By organizing them into general categories there emerge four pillars upon which true liberty is created, established, and maintained:

- **First Pillar**: A moral code universally taught and voluntarily practiced. The Bible is the basis for America's Moral Code.

- **Second Pillar**: A written set of governing principles and laws the people have agreed to honor. America's principles are written in the Declaration of Independence, the Constitution, and all laws standing in harmony with these.

- **Third Pillar**: An economic system where rights to property are protected, there is sound money, and there is freedom to try, buy, sell, and fail. America's Constitution provides all of these.

- **Fourth Pillar**: A devotion among the people to help the nation succeed as demonstrated by their willingness to be industrious and to obey the laws. The Framers called this Virtue.

The sequence of the four pillars is deliberate. The Moral Code must come first because the Constitution cannot transform a corrupt people into saints and angels. While Americans are working to save their Constitution, they must simultaneously be working to restore their traditional Moral Code.

Review Questions

1. What is People's Law? Can you name some ways People's Law has become corrupted in America?

2. Considering the "three-headed eagle," and the role of "left wing" and "right wing," can you give examples of how the government is not working in harmony to solve America's biggest problems? For your examples, which wing or head is not doing its job? What should it be doing instead?

3. Why did the Framers place so much importance on strong, local self-government?

4. How important is the family in preserving America? How important is education to preserve the American culture?

5. What specific problems have erupted in American culture as a consequence of the serious deterioration of family in the last two generations?

6. Sir William Blackstone described the role of the community in establishing public morals. What are some examples of private moral choices that today have been imposed on communities in the name of "equality" or a "constitutional right"? Has this helped or hurt America's culture? Explain.

7. What are the four pillars of self-government? Which pillar do you believe has suffered the greatest corruption? Which of the pillars will be the most difficult to restore?

STEP 3

RESTORE THE
FIRST PILLAR:
THE MORAL CODE

Identify the Moral Code in the Ten Commandments and the Sermon on the Mount.

Adopt the suggestions and ideas to restore the Moral Code.

Preview

Laws alone do not a great country make. It is the people and their ability to live together in harmony and industrious cooperation that make a country great. Protecting the people from criminal behavior and corruption requires there be guardians. It is impractical, however, to put a police officer in every home and at every street corner. True self-government therefore requires every individual to be self-governed, to put moral chains on their human passions. Maturing to this level of personal responsibility isn't natural. It must be taught and defended from generation to generation.

CHAPTER 11

The First Pillar: A Universal Moral Code

here is no question about where the Framers' turned to identify America's moral values. They called it the well-spring of truth for everlasting self-government.[99]

"The Bible is a book which teaches man his own individual responsibility, his own dignity, and his equality with his fellow-men," said Daniel Webster (1843), an early defender of the Constitution. "And it is not to be doubted that the free and universal reading of the Bible is to be ascribed, in that age, that men were indebted for right views of Civil Liberty."[100]

Noah Webster, a soldier in the revolution, said in 1832, "The moral principles and precepts found in the Scriptures ought to form the basis of all our civil constitutions and laws."

To this he added sometime later, "All the ... evils which men suffer from vice, crime, ambition, injustice, oppression, slavery and war, proceed from their despising or neglecting the precepts contained in the Bible."[101]

Benjamin Rush who helped ratify the Constitution, pointed out in 1830 that "The Bible contains more knowledge necessary to man in his present state than any other book in the world."[102]

Where in the Bible are These Values Presented?

The laws and statutes making up America's common values may be found concentrated in several preeminent books of the Bible.

The starting place is the Ten Commandments in Exodus 20 and Deuteronomy 5. An additional 100 statutes, sometimes called God's Law or Natural Law, are concentrated primarily in Exodus chapters 20–31, Leviticus chapters 7–25, Numbers chapters 11–39, Deuteronomy chapters 11–25, and in a handful of chapters nearby.[103] Beautiful refinements to those values are in the Sermon on the Mount given by Jesus and recorded in Matthew 5–7. Linked to these values are examples, parables, and stories that validate their usefulness for running an orderly society.

Personal Governance is the Key to Liberty

Religion's one great purpose is to teach self-governance, or better said, obedience to God's Law. Said Paul to Timothy, "For if a man know not how to rule his own house, how shall he take care of the church of God?"[104] (1 Timothy 3:5)

In other words, if people are not self-controlled in their private lives, how can they be trusted in marriage, parenthood, friendships, business relations, contracts, or political leadership?

Edmund Burke made it clear: "Men are qualified for civil liberty in exact proportion to their disposition to put moral chains upon their own appetites ... the less of it there is within, the more there must be without. It is ordained in the eternal constitution of things, that men of intemperate minds cannot be free. Their passions forge their fetters."[105] Eventually, all people must learn right from wrong.

The Test of Right and Wrong

Right and wrong are moral principles that do not change. The Bible best teaches these principles, and reading it is how to convey this standard to the people. Albert E. Bowen pointed out that "...we cannot well lay claim to being a grown-up, mature, civilized people until we have come to the point where morality is the determinant, and we ask simply what is, in good conscience, right. The conclusion seems inescapable that the confusion and distraction and conflicts and antagonisms and uncertainties and bewilderment which plague the world today present mankind with what is at the bottom a purely moral issue—the issue between right and wrong. That, then, should be the final test of the propriety of all courses of action." [106]

Virtue and Values Presume Religion

A society devoid of true religion, or knowledge of right and wrong, is doomed to collapse. Gouverneur Morris, the author of the "Preamble to the Constitution," explained in 1816, "There must be religion. When that ligament is torn, society is disjointed and its members perish ... The most important of all lessons is the denunciation [public condemnation] of ruin to every state that rejects the precepts of religion." [107]

Richard Henry Lee was prophetic about the collapse of morals that comes when there is no religion, when he wrote to James Madison in 1784, "Refiners may weave as fine a web of reason as they please, but the experience of all times shews Religion to be the guardian of morals." [108]

Religion Based on the Bible

Religion that is founded on the correct principles in the Bible is inseparably fused with the Constitution. John Adams said in 1798 the Constitution works only "for a moral and religious people. It is wholly inadequate to the government of any other." [109] After examining all religions for truth about freedom, he concluded "the Bible is the best book in the world." [110]

Samuel Adams said in 1748 that neither the "wisest constitution nor the wisest laws will secure the liberty and happiness of a people whose manners are universally corrupt." [111]

Thomas Jefferson cautioned that freedom depends on sincere

religious practice to survive: "And can the liberties of a nation be thought secure when we have removed their only firm basis, a conviction in the minds of the people that these liberties are the gift of God? That they are not to be violated but with his wrath? Indeed I tremble for my country when I reflect that God is just: that his justice cannot sleep for ever...."[112]

John Adams admonished Americans to make religion an active part of their lives: "It is the duty of all men in society, publicly, and at stated seasons, to worship the Supreme Being, the great Creator and Preserver of the universe. And no subject shall be hurt, molested, or restrained, in his person, liberty, or estate, for worshiping God in the manner most agreeable to the dictates of his own conscience; or for his religious profession or sentiments; provided he doth not disturb the public peace, or obstruct others in their religious worship."[113]

Religion is a Property Right

James Madison explained in 1792 that a person's right to think abstractly and practice it as he pleases, doing no harm to others, is as real and palpable a right as the right to property. He said that whatever a person attaches value to is his own property and must be protected by law. He included among these rights a person's opinions, his right to communicate them, and his private religious beliefs. He said "Conscience is the most sacred of all property."[114]

"Must I Convert?"

Former Secretary of Agriculture Ezra Taft Benson astutely observed, "You can't do wrong and feel right. It's impossible."[115]

As America works to re-establish its Biblical Moral Code, the obvious question arises: Must a person be a practicing Jew or a converted Christian to live America's Moral Code and avoid "doing wrong"?

The equally obvious answer is: No, of course not. Any person of any faith, including atheism, will benefit by living this Bible-based Moral Code. Aligning with a particular sect certainly helps, and the Framers encouraged that, but it isn't mandatory in order to live by these values.

George Washington beautifully summed up the Framers' view of the free exercise of conscience in 1789: "I have often expressed my sentiments, that every man, conducting himself as a good citizen, and being accountable to God alone for his religious opinions, ought to be protected in worshiping the Deity according to the dictates of his own conscience...[116] No man who is profligate in his morals, or a bad member of the civil community, can possibly be a true Christian or a credit to his own religious society."[117]

The power of the Moral Code is that it restricts the harm bad men may cause, yet does not depend on finding good men to run things. Instead, as F. A. Hayek said in 1948, the liberties guaranteed by the Constitution "makes use of men in all their given variety and complexity, sometimes good and sometimes bad, sometimes intelligent and more often stupid. [The Framers'] aim was a system under which it should be possible to grant freedom to all."[118]

The Moral Code is Inseparable from Religion

Washington saw religion as central to sustaining and perpetuating the Moral Code: "Let us with caution indulge the supposition, that Morality can be maintained without religion... reason and experience both forbid us to expect that national morality can prevail in exclusion of religious principles."[119]

Never by Force or Compulsion

Although religion is vital to sustaining the Moral Code, for dozens of centuries, even to this very day, religion has also been used as a tool of tyranny and bloodshed. Religion in America was never intended to create conformists, but instead, to create the right environment where people can have faith in one another and in their mutual aspirations. The freedom of conscience, religion, and human rights must all share in the same lawful protections.

Finding the Moral Code in the Bible

In 1800, Charles Carroll was prophetic when he said attacks on the Christian religion in his day were a direct assault on liberty and human rights. It is the same today:

"Without morals a republic cannot subsist any length of time; they therefore, who are decrying the Christian religion, whose morality is so sublime and pure, which ... insures to the good eternal happiness, are undermining the solid foundation of morals, the best security for the duration of free government." [120]

Therein may be found the universal standard to which all people may safely unite. The Framers saw in the Bible over any other text the best vehicle for conveying from one generation to the next that universal standard of proper behavior: A principle-based universal Moral Code.

CHAPTER 12

Finding the Moral Code in The Ten Commandments

t takes less than ten minutes to read both versions of the Ten Commandments. These statements establish the starting place for America's common values.

The Bible and a Universal Moral Code

The Framers made it clear that their vision of a constitutional representative government would not work for a corrupted people. They took hope in the fact that most Americans were raised with Biblical values. They believed if these true principles would be popularly taught then the new nation would have a fighting chance of succeeding.

The Three Laws

Throughout his writings, Moses constantly refers to the Law of the Covenant or God's law in three parts:

First, the Commandments: The famous Decalogue of Ten Commandments was given to Moses in the presence of all of Israel at the foot of Mount Sinai and later inscribed on two stone tables by the finger of God.

Second, the Statutes: These are God's laws that John Adams called the "divine science" of good government for happy living and the complete formula for an ideal society. There are about 100 statutes describing how to deal with issues such as accidental homicide, kidnapping, battery, mayhem, treatment of animals, the liability of uncovered wells or pits, killing burglars, liability from wandering animals, arson, breach of trust, seduction, treatment of widows and orphans, loans and interest, bearing false witness, mobs, bribery, abusing the poor, land use, festivals, celebrations, idolatry, and so on.[121]

Third, the Judgments: There are the two kinds of judgments that God has held in reserve—rewards for the righteous who deserve "blessings" and "punishments" for those who haven't qualified themselves for blessings.

The Ten Commandments reflect on two important relationships:

1. The divine relationship between God and man (the first four Commandments, typically numbered 1–4).

2. The divine relationship that we have with one another as God's children (the six Commandments numbered 5–10).

Read The Ten Commandments

The two versions of the Ten Commandments are found in Exodus 20 and Deuteronomy 5.

Deuteronomy 5:1 And Moses called all Israel, and said unto them, Hear, O Israel, the statutes and judgments which I speak in your ears this day, that ye may learn them, and keep, and do them.

This opening declaration is important because Moses said *these commandments are eternal and immutable laws upon which a free and orderly society is built.* Israel was commanded to take them seriously, to learn them, to keep them, and to do them. It was God's action plan for freedom.

I. Thou shalt have no other gods before me.

The Moral Code: There is only one true law and anything more or less than this will fail.

God represents true order, harmony, and balance in the universe. His natural laws govern all things on two levels. The lower law governs the physical universe that is described, understood, and predicted by science.

The higher law manages the moral conduct of individuals who share the same unalienable rights. Their free-will independence is governed by the degree to which they honor those rights in others. Cultures practicing the higher law enjoy more peace, prosperity, and freedom than cultures practicing lesser forms. [122]

As stated in the Declaration of Independence, America's Moral Code honors and sustains the Laws of Nature and of Nature's God. [123]

2. Thou shalt not make unto thee any graven image.

The Moral Code: Principles reign supreme, not men.

Graven images in modern terms are those things that steer people away from the Laws of Nature and Nature's God. It is the worship of materialism, and it's on display as brazen adulation and deification of the works of fellow humans. The worship of these false gods appears as vanity, fads, pride, envy, greed, hero worship, fawning over media stars, moral indiscretions, addictions, lust, today's cultural attitude of "anything goes" and "eat, drink, and be merry, for tomorrow we die." Modern-day graven images have led many millions away from the true principles of Natural Law. They are today's equivalent of ancient Israel's Golden Calf and all of the human foibles and decay that are associated with it.

America's Moral Code promotes the *principles* of prosperity, not the *fruits* of prosperity. As a culture descends into corruption, having a great accumulation of possessions, prestige, and power—the fruits—is more important to them than serving and helping their fellow beings. It is unrestrained vanity.

3. Thou shalt not take the name of the Lord thy God in vain.

The Moral Code: Personal oaths are imperative for managing imperfect humans at their most sacred and critically essential level.

Originally an oath was the supreme solemn act of covenant-making. When a person stands in court and swears to "tell the truth, the whole truth, and nothing but the truth, so help me God," he is under the injunction of the Almighty that the name of God is not to be taken in vain.

The American founding fathers believed that we should hold these oaths and covenants sacred and conscientiously fulfill them or the judgment of the Almighty would hold us responsible. Of equal moral consequences is an affirmation to fulfill a promise, used by some religions and by those of no faith–"I swear or affirm that .... "

If each person honored every sacred promise made in the name of Deity our courts would provide a hundred times more justice, our business life would be a great deal more honest, and the administration of public affairs would be much more efficient.

4. Remember the Sabbath day to keep it holy.

The Moral Code: A day of rest for religious worship and service encourages prudent management of human resources.

The institutions of Sabbath Day worship keep the Hebrew and Christian cultures healthy in America. Abolishing the observance of the Sabbath Day by changing it from a holy day to a holiday has gone far in nullifying its positive impact on American society.

Often overlooked regarding a day of rest are those tender parts of life that are usually neglected during the busy week. These include undivided time with spouse and children, serving others, tending to the needs of the sick and elderly, remembering God, visiting neighbors, and building strong community bonds.

A part of America's Moral Code is to help our neighbors, to serve others, to slow down and take stock of our mortality, to wind down the angst of day-to-day struggle by taking a regular weekly Sabbath. It is a pattern of happy living on which America's original social order was built.

5. Honor thy Father and Mother.

The Moral Code: Strong family solidarity makes for a strong and cohesive nation.

America's strength is in its families. These are the primary channels through which the Moral Code is best delivered. By example and guidance, parents teach the rising generation the finer qualities of humanity. This builds love, empathy, compassionate service, and familial cohesion. There are lessons of life to be shared, a personal witness to the fruits of good choices and bad fruits of mistakes. The family is the best delivery channel for a proven moral code to be passed from one generation to the next.

America's winning Moral Code blesses the rising generation when such values are safely transferred with love, patience, and teaching from father and mother to son and daughter.

6. Thou shalt not kill.

The Moral Code: Human life is the only asset in mortality with true intrinsic value and must be protected.

No individual has the moral authority to take the life of another except in self-defense, defense of another, or in meting out justice for capital crimes. With the decline of America's common values and Moral Code, the nation finds itself today in a period where killing is losing the important stigma once attached to it, be it in criminal gang killings, crimes, abortion, revenge, assisted suicide, euthanasia, or even in removing capital punishment as the ultimate act of justice supporting the sanctity of innocent life.

By reestablishing this commandment as part of an overall emphasis on the sanctity of life, America's Moral Code will prevent untold numbers of problems, agonies, and controversies that run rampant today. There waits for every human being a future court of justice that is less tolerant of the excuses and rationalizations offered by many who extinguish innocent life as a matter of course.

7. Thou shalt not commit adultery.

The Moral Code: The traditional family is the first group, the building block, the living strength of America, and it must be preserved.

The traditional family is the basic unit of society. Keeping the family intact rests upon trust at the most intimate levels. Moral integrity does not begin with marriage. It finds its strength in careful self-discipline over the years that precede marriage.

After spouses commit to a companionship built on covenants of the sincerest form, there is no greater insurance for a life of happiness and trust than a couple that is able to say to each other, "Even before I knew you, I honored you and kept myself circumspect for you."

Practitioners of Marxism, humanism, secularism, and communism recognize the family as society's great powerhouse of cultural strength and persistence. Therefore, the family is their single greatest hindrance to achieving political supremacy. Discrediting the family and the institutions that support them are revealed by a culture that encourages promiscuity, pornography, abortion, and gives quarter to aberrations of normal human sexuality, co-habitation, easy divorce, and dilutes the social stigma against adultery, fornication, premarital sex, and perversion.

A strong Moral Code is meaningless without strong families and pure fidelity in marriage.

8. That shalt not steal.

The Moral Code: The role of government is to protect private property.

In the corrupted corners of American society, this commandment has been rephrased as "Thou shalt not get caught stealing."

One of the main purposes of government is the protection of private property. The fruit of people's labors, their tangible or creative property, is a projection of their very lives onto the world. The vast majority of benefits people enjoy in life are the consequences of somebody's creative hard work that was encouraged by the promise they could own and develop their property, and profit from it.

Theft of such property removes profits, incentives, and the very means and ability to create things beneficial to others. Stealing property hurts individuals and entire generations. Communism and socialism are two economic systems where private property is confiscated and distributed to others. These systems have and always will fail because they violate a person's right to property, and basic economic principles.

For America's vibrant and prosperous culture to remain, its Moral Code must protect private property and intellectual rights.

9. Thou shalt not bear false witness.

The Moral Code: The well-being of the community is best served by individual truthfulness across all venues and in all circumstances.

Aside from all the good that modern social media has brought in bounteous quantities and forms, character assassination has become an American pastime. This includes deception, insinuation, lying, or withholding information for political gain or cultural change through the great gossip channel of social media. These actions of "false witness" never needed social media to be spread among the people, but the Communications Age has given the speed of light to so much mud-throwing and muckraking. Modern-day terrorists use the Internet to spread fear and horror. Paid political demonstrators use it to destroy people their sponsors don't like. Activists use it to incite the passionate youth and politically illiterate into meaningless demonstrations of chaos against this value or that, this person or that group, all for the camera and fame.

An orderly society must be governed according to laws the people establish. For justice to render the laws with any effect, a commitment to truthfulness on every level of society must be cultivated. In ancient Israel a person found lying to the judges would be sentenced to the penalties he hoped would be heaped on the person he wanted found guilty of a crime.[124] America's Moral Code includes the aspiration toward integrity and personal fortitude to divulge truthfully the facts to which he or she is privy.

10. Thou shalt not covet.

The Moral Code: "We reap what we sow."

This is a paraphrase of Paul the Apostle who told the Galatians, "For every man shall bear his own burden. Whatsoever a man soweth, that shall he also reap."[125] Coveting is desiring to harvest what another person has sowed. It is a basic law of nature that every capable individual is responsible to build his or her own life, and to become a contributor to the betterment of their family, community, and world. A strong work ethic taught to children beginning at an early age builds resilience in the individual adult, and builds power in the nation.

The desire to want good things is not a sin. But to acquire them by cheating or extorting them from a neighbor is both a sin and a crime.

Envy, greed, and lust are all forms of coveting. Left unchecked these negative desires can drive people to break laws, break morality, break trust, and break hearts.

An unintended consequence of America's prosperity is the creation of status and conformity as a cultural measurement of value and self-worth. It is coveting and vanity of the worst kind to judge as worthless the true intrinsic value of another human being using the shallow guides of appearance, poverty, or status.

The cure for vanity and covetousness is a change of heart. The happiest people adopt a charitable spirit of service and good work ethics. That becomes the focus of their lives instead of dwelling on possessing the property, the relationships, or the status of others.

CHAPTER 13

Finding the Moral Code in the
Sermon on the Mount

J esus delivered his famous Sermon on the Mount early in his ministry. It is his longest continuous quote (recorded in the Matthew, chapters 5, 6, and 7) and includes some of his most famous teachings, including the Beatitudes and The Lord's Prayer.

Dealing with Human Nature

Jesus had the highest aspirations for the human family. He wanted all of mankind to become a beautiful people and to perfect themselves in righteousness.

However, Jesus knew that the dangerous pathway that winds and twists up through mortality is steep, and the road is rocky. The main problem to be dealt with is "human nature." Of course, we "inherited" our human nature. It is carefully structured on a foundation of God-given and in-born instincts, specifically designed to help us survive.

In a sense, these survival instincts are built-in resources which turn out to be powerful desires, emotions, and demands that our physical bodies constantly impose upon us.

For example, they demand that we eat. They demand that we drink. They demand that we be comfortable—not too much heat, not too much cold, not too hard, and not too soft. They demand that we satisfy certain appetites. They demand that we satisfy certain tastes and abhor others. They demand that we seek out a certain pleasant scent but treat other smells with disdain. They demand that others like us. They demand that we avenge ourselves on those who don't like us. They demand that we satisfy our sexuality. They demand that we get things, and get them in quantity. The list goes on and on.

These instincts begin before birth and most of them last until we die.

The problem with all of these instincts is that while they are important for our survival they get in the way of spiritual growth, long-term happiness, and living in a free society of self-government.

Therefore, every human being is confronted with a dilemma. God and nature give us a set of survival instincts, and then morality tells us to subdue them in order to get along with others, achieve peace, and maintain harmony in society. When those instincts are not subdued, women's rights are destroyed, minority rights are destroyed, children are subjected to horrors, and the ravages of conflict and war always erupt to spread misery, terror, and death.

So, all through our earth-life, there is a war going on between the spirit and the flesh. The Framers wondered, could a nation be built on the premise that its citizens would be positively engaged in this battle against human nature and eventually win it, or at least subdue it, for the betterment of themselves and everyone else? That is the hopeful message of the Sermon on the Mount.

Christians and non-Christians alike can benefit from the simple statements Jesus made in his famous sermon. His most profound messages about promoting responsible free will and acting with honesty toward others is a standard to which people of all beliefs can rally.

Christianity and the Constitution

The Founding Generation was raised in a Christian culture and belief system. They firmly believed the Gospel of Jesus Christ was more conducive, protective, and accommodating to free will and liberty than any other system—religious or not. The Sermon finishes the work started in the Old Testament to establish a reliable Moral Code independent of religious affiliations. [126]

Framers Acknowledge Christianity

In 1809, Thomas Jefferson cited the Sermon as sitting at the heart of liberty:

"The practice of morality being necessary for the wellbeing of society, He [God] has taken care to impress its precepts so indelibly on our hearts that they shall not be effaced [erased] by the subtleties of our brain. We all agree in the obligation of the moral principles of Jesus and nowhere will they be found delivered in greater purity than in His discourses." [127]

To this he added, "The doctrines of Jesus are simple, and tend all to the happiness of man."

Patrick Henry lauded Christianity's role in establishing liberty.

"Righteousness alone can exalt [America] as a nation. ...Whoever thou art, remember this; and in thy sphere practice virtue thyself, and encourage it in others." [128]

The Best Values for Civil Society

Benjamin Franklin said in 1790, "As to Jesus of Nazareth, my opinion of whom you particularly desire, I think the system of morals and His religion as He left them to us, [are] the best the world ever saw or is likely to see." [129]

Joseph Story who served on the first Supreme Court, said "I verily believe that Christianity is necessary to support a civil society and shall ever attend to its institutions and acknowledge its precepts as the pure and natural sources of private and social happiness."[130]

A Success Formula to be Shared and Taught

George Washington counseled his soldiers that in addition to building "the distinguished character of Patriot, it should be our highest glory to add the more distinguished character of Christian."[131]

In comments to a group of Delaware Chiefs in 1779, Washington advised, "You do well to wish to learn our arts and ways of life, and above all, the religion of Jesus Christ. These will make you a greater and happier people than you are."[132]

Best Source of Wisdom, Virtue, Equity

In 1796, John Adams said "The Christian religion is, above all the religions that ever prevailed or existed in ancient or modern times, the religion of wisdom, virtue, equity and humanity."[133]

John Hancock said in 1780, "Sensible of the importance of Christian piety and virtue to the order and happiness of a state, I cannot but earnestly commend to you every measure for their support and encouragement."[134]

Christianity is the Cornerstone

John Quincy Adams said in 1837 that "in the chain of human events, the birthday of the nation is indissolubly linked with the birthday of the Savior. The Declaration of Independence laid the cornerstone of human government upon the first precepts of Christianity."[135]

A signer of the Declaration, Benjamin Rush, said in 1807 that "by renouncing the Bible, philosophers swing from their moorings upon all moral subjects ... It is the only correct map of the human heart that ever has been published."[136] He added, "The great enemy of the salvation of man, in my opinion, never invented a more effective means of limiting

Christianity from the world than by persuading mankind that it was improper to read the Bible at schools." [137]

Civil Liberty Connected to Voluntary Bible Reading

Daniel Webster, an early defender of the Constitution, said in 1843: "...to the free and universal reading of the Bible... men [are] much indebted for right views of civil liberty." [138]

Noah Webster, a soldier in the revolutionary war, said in 1832: "... the moral principles and precepts found in the Scriptures ought to form the basis of all our civil constitutions and laws." Later on he said "All the miseries and evils which men suffer from vice, crime, ambition, injustice, oppression, slavery and war, proceed from their despising or neglecting the precepts contained in the Bible." [139]

Benjamin Rush, a ratifier of the Constitution, pointed out that "The Bible contains more knowledge necessary to man in his present state than any other book in the world."

He also cautioned that "The Bible, when not read in schools, is seldom read in any subsequent period of life... [T]he Bible... should be read in our schools in preference to all other books because it contains the greatest portion of that kind of knowledge which is calculated to produce private and public happiness." [140]

Importance of Reading the Sermon on the Mount

Voluntary religion helps a people regulate themselves in the rules of self-government. People learn from a young age to respect law, order, justice, and the unalienable rights of others for reasons that are enduring and spiritually valid. It makes for better policing of the heart.

Therefore, take time today to read the Sermon on the Mount in Matthew 5, 6, and 7. Most people can read it in about 30 minutes.

Dictators Forbid Freedom of Conscience

Tyrants throughout history have tightly regulated the free-will act of religious belief. The Bible tells of Daniel being thrown into the lions' den for breaking a law by praying to God.[141] His three friends, Shadrach, Meshach, and Abednego, were thrown into a fiery furnace for not bowing down before a pagan image of gold.[142] Jesus paid with his life for exercising his right to speak the greatest truths of all, as did most of his Apostles. This illustrates the danger that tyrants pose regardless of the many forms in which they appear: Mobs, religious zealots, fanatics, bullies, elitists, academics, kings, judges, politicians, administrators, and so on.

Although Daniel and his friends were spared a terrible death through miraculous interventions, this is rarely the outcome for millions of others who are oppressed, abused, executed, or murdered because of their religious beliefs. In this modern age the harassment and killing of people because of their personal faith and conscience continues in the most severe and horrific ways.

National Decay Begins with Institutional Decay

While a perfect Constitution won't transform a rotten people into a righteous people, a crumbling Constitution will certainly transform a good people into rotten as anarchy, chaos, disorder, panic, and desperation bring out the very worst in people.

Religion in America has played an essential role in retaining an orderly society. It has served to bind people together—a cultural connective tissue in the form of marriage, family, churches, organized religions, service organizations, the town hall sense of belonging, and the erection of standing monuments to the high watermarks of achievements in our historical past. The old saying holds true that united we stand, divided we fall. Actively religious people help America stand united, and Jesus's Sermon on the Mount points the way. It's how we'll save the Constitution.

CHAPTER 14

Gems of Liberty from the Sermon on the Mount

Searching for liberty in the Sermon on the Mount breathes hope into a world filled with darkness, pain, and conflict. Throughout his sermon, Jesus identified several dozen eternal truths that form the foundation of good government. Here are some highlights:

Matthew 5:1–11, The Beatitudes

Moral Code: National Virtue is not possible without individual virtue.

Jesus begins his sermon with the Beatitudes, a list of difficulties that most people will experience if they live long enough. He promises that during such hardships, by turning to him for strength and enduring well, the experiences will become a blessing in people's lives. "Come unto me, all ye that . . . are heavy laden"[143] means to adopt his principles for living life with the positives of virtue, love, mercy, compassion, forgiveness, service, industry, endurance, patience, repentance, personal prayer, and spirituality.[144]

The Framers based their structure of self-government on the premise that achieving mastery over the flesh is essential to achieving self-government as a nation. Such mastery is conquering the natural human instincts that lead to conflict, disorder, and distrust. This self-cleansing results in individuals who are improved, refined, and happy. A nation determined to govern itself as a whole must first become a people determined to govern themselves as individuals.

Matthew 5:12–16, "Ye are the salt of the earth … Let your light so shine"[145]

Moral Code: Virtuous leaders are essential to maintaining liberty.

Leadership was one of the first concerns Jesus addressed because righteous leaders are always in short supply. He told his disciples that as leaders they must remember "Ye are the salt of the earth" sent among the people to both preserve and season—that is, to teach and strengthen. Leaders must be valiant in the long run and never lose their savor. America's Founding Generation was active in promoting this counsel, striving regularly to keep the Bible's teachings central: "Let your light so shine before men."

Matthew 5:21–32, "Thou shalt not kill … Thou shalt not commit adultery"

Moral Code: Murder and adultery destroy the fabric of liberty.

Jesus elaborated on two of the most serious offenses that have led countless people and nations into collapse: Murder and moral decadence. Both are the products of premeditation. Diffusing arguments early, avoiding offensive words, and refusing to lust after others are disciplines that circumvent possible tragedy and build both mature human beings and a morally strong nation.[146]

Jesus took those same issues a step further, saying that grudges against others can simmer and stew until contention and hatred boil over. The Framers recognized that the power of individuals working hard to self-police their hearts is far more effective than posting actual police officers to keep good order in society. Jesus counseled the people to "first be reconciled to thy brother" before assuming an attitude of humility before God—go apologize or make amends first. An orderly society is the result of being other-oriented in this way, to love others as you love yourself.[147]

Matthew 5:27–32, "If thy right eye offend thee, pluck it out"
Moral Code: Religion, morality, and knowledge are the keys to happiness and good government.

A Jewish custom in the days of Jesus was to make reference to a teacher or leader or guide as an eye, foot, or hand leading others along paths of understanding. However, if those "eyes," "feet" or "hands" led people down wrong paths, Jesus said pluck them out or cut them off. The Framers adopted that concept in the Northwest Ordinance where they said "good government and the happiness of mankind" could be developed by teaching the people "Religion, morality and knowledge."[148]

Matthew 5:33–37, "Swear not at all . . . Let your communications be Yea, yea; Nay, nay"[149]
Moral Code: Honest oaths and respectful language support equality.

Taking an oath had become casual and meaningless among the Jews in the days of Jesus. Jesus made the taking of an oath very sacred because an oath is taken in the name of God. As already discussed in the Ten Commandments, oath-taking is essential to important parts of life: Holding true to covenants, telling the truth in court, putting one's life on the line for the Constitution, political office, and so on. This included Jesus' concern about pollution of the language. Oaths should be sacred, offensive words should not be used—show respect toward others even if they are an enemy. "Swear not at all," Jesus said about secular endorsements.[150]

Offensive language can lead to social unrest on a small scale that can escalate to rioting and mob action on a larger scale. On one occasion Jesus said, "But those things which proceed out of the mouth come forth from the heart; and they defile the man."[151] On these gentle words the Framers wanted to build America where a person's words could be trusted to embody truth, integrity, and respect for all others.

Matthew 5:38–42, "An eye for an eye, a tooth for a tooth"

Moral Code: True liberty is marked by rule of law, not rule by people.

The idea of "an eye for an eye, a tooth for a tooth" is better understood as "the value of an eye for an eye, the value of a tooth for a tooth." Compensating the victim with some form of reparation did more to restore the victim's loss than would angry vengeance or mob action by having the perpetrator's eye or tooth removed. [152]

For murder there was no compensation or reparation possible. The killer had to forfeit his own life because his is of no greater value than the life he took: "He shall surely be put to death." [153] The Framers created a judicial system based on the due process of law whereby every citizen was given equal protection. The Bill of Rights secures "rule by law," not rule by mobs, vigilantes, or by biased and prejudicial people. [154]

Matthew 5:43–48, "Love your enemies ... do good to them that hate you"

Moral Code: Common-sense civility helps mitigate human failings.

Loving an enemy, blessing those that curse you, doing good to those that hate you, and praying for persecutors are indeed contrary to every human instinct. Yet the Framers adopted this attitude on several levels in America, from being innocent unless proven guilty, to forgiving and resolving conflicts on a national or international scale. Even when justified to strike back or do damage, Jesus's counsel to first consider the long term impact of taking certain actions has served Americans well. Wanting to help an enemy isn't easy and can be abused by clever adversaries. But in the end, the best kind of love is reciprocal love, and that is the goal—to change an enemy into a loving friend. [155]

Matthew 7:12, "Do unto others as you would have them do unto you" [156]

Moral Code: Become respected by first being respectful.

Jesus's Golden Rule [157] is the great rudder that constantly steers self-government toward the equilibrium of natural law. Every law should be tested with this question: "Will this do good unto me as well as it will do good unto others?"

This compassion and consideration requires the most vigorous self discipline to enact. While it is not an easy rule to live by, it is the most rewarding. Any person who masters this mode of life is living on the level of the prophets of God. The Framers knew that America's system of self-government would always give birth to good laws conforming to natural law if they first had to pass this test of the Golden Rule.

Matthew 6:5–15, "When thou prayest ... pray to thy Father which is in secret"

Moral Code: Humble, prayerful, and teachable people qualify themselves for God's multitude of blessings.

Next to his atoning sacrifice, Jesus's greatest mission was to help turn all of us from our human flaws of being self-centered toward building a loving relationship with our Father in Heaven. That closeness could be developed through private and earnest prayer. Jesus taught that the portals of heaven could be opened on the basis of humility, child-like obedience, kindness of the most sincere form, a broken heart, a contrite spirit, and a continuing state of repentance. "Use not vain repetitions, as the heathen do," Jesus said, but be comforted in the knowledge that "your Father knoweth what things ye have need of, before ye ask him." [158]

The Framers were no strangers to prayer. Their petitions to God for help during their greatest struggles are well documented. A nation of prayerful people is more resilient and powerful than the world's most dominant forces. On that basis the Framers hoped the people would keep their personal lives and interactions on the highest plain of behavior. Personal communion with God through sincere and private prayer is the foundation of America's miraculous past, amazing present, and sensational future.

Matthew 6:1–18, "Be not as the hypocrites ... They have their reward"

Moral Code: An attitude of generosity and humility lifts everyone.

Jesus wanted his followers to approach all things with humility and kindness. He cautioned the people never to use opportunities of service or prayer as a means to show off or exalt themselves above others. "When thou doest alms, let ... thine alms ... be in secret." And regarding prayer, to pray in secret, and "use not vain repetitions." And when fasting, "be not, as the hypocrites, of a sad countenance; for they disfigure their faces, that they may appear unto men to fast. Verily I say unto you, they have their reward."

In this wise counsel the Framers found several cautions about granting elected officers in the new government the means of building their own little kingdoms. Their approach was to make such offices places of honor, not profit. [159]

Matthew 7:1–6, "Judge not, that ye be not judged" [160]

Moral Code: Due process starts with "Innocent until proven guilty."

Everyone judges, all of the time—they must and they should. It's all a part of making wise and proper decisions. The key word that is missing in this version of Jesus's counsel is "unrighteously." People should never judge another unrighteously. In support of that merciful assessment of the actions by others, there is a another aspect of judging to consider.

Living in a system of law and justice means no one is above the law. If inequality is allowed to preside, the whole system of self-government will collapse. Jesus declared that those who judge will be judged by the same judgment. The Framers acknowledged this common sense call to fairness as essential. The Bill of Rights grew out of the concept that no one is above the law. When justice requires formal judging it must proceed according to due process, in righteousness, and with an assumption of innocence. Equality under the law is the sure sign of true liberty.

Matthew 7:7–12, "Knock, and it shall be opened unto you"

Moral Code: The free pursuit of knowledge and self-interest is the engine of innovation, prosperity, and economic growth.

Jesus revealed one of his great disappointments when his choice servants lose their spiritual curiosity. They became satisfied with a *little* when they could have *a lot*. "Ask, and it shall be given you," he promised. "Seek, and ye shall find; knock, and it shall be opened unto you." [161]

From the Framer's perspective, only in self-government and liberty could this spirit of curiosity be cultivated. It is a necessary ingredient to prevent the government from becoming the answer to all things. The so-called nanny state, created to provide all necessities from cradle to grave, is good only for coddling. Such Utopian ideas always create stagnation, complacency, and economic collapse.

Life is consistently delivering surprises. The free market can act on those surprises to build, create, invent, lift, and prosper. Socialism assumes there can be no more surprises, that humanity's sole purpose is to manage the existing levels of prosperity and make it fair. And on that sour philosophy have nations fallen to ashes. Jesus therefore admonished his followers to keep asking, seeking, and knocking—these are the golden threads leading to liberty, peace, and prosperity.

Jesus' challenge is to build a life instead of just living a life, to knock and to seek. It is the central ingredient to the enthusiasm the Framers unitedly encouraged for America. It was self-evident to them that a spirit of curiosity unleashed into a free market would serve all of mankind in the best way possible. If a person can't ask, seek, or knock, it is a certainty that such a person also won't receive, find, or pass through unopened doors.

A person who may "knock" and "seek" without government interference is in a true state of liberty.

Matthew 7:13–14, "Narrow is the way, which leadeth unto life ... few there be that find it"

Moral Code: Liberty isn't inherited, it must be upheld, confirmed, and defended daily.

"Enter ye in at the strait gate," Jesus said, "for wide is the gate, and broad is the way, that leadeth to destruction."[162]

There are two roads that stand open for every human being who reaches the age of accountability: The strait road to growth and prosperity, or the wide and easy road to stagnation, consumption, and squandering opportunities for nothing.

Jesus wanted everyone who heard his messages to enter in at the "strait gate," which in terms of Christianity is repentance and baptism for the remission of sins.

The word "strait" means difficult, demanding, and exacting. Jesus said the strait gate might be narrow but it opens into a vast expanse of limitless possibilities which he called everlasting life.

The same can be said of liberty. Only when the people voluntarily submit themselves to the demanding and exact Laws of Nature and of Nature's God can they enjoy lasting liberty. Anything less than that leads to the broad and easy gate of subservience to others, a wasted life–despondency, addictions, enslavement, and despair.

The Framers acknowledged this failing in human nature, and wrote into the Constitution numerous barriers to help the nation advance along that narrow way without violating human rights. It depended on the willingness of each individual to strive to live the higher law that Jesus taught.

Matthew 7:15–20, "By their fruits ye shall know them"[163]

Moral Code: Prove all things by their fruits.

Who are the false prophets in self-government? Purveyors of false principles have been the most destructive influence through the ages, those who have risen among the people with their so-called "better way" ideas.

These are the false prophets Jesus was referring to, the false messiahs, the false politicians, the false teachers, the wicked miscreants dressed in godly raiment and the elitist robes of superiority who prey upon the unsuspecting masses. Jesus lumped them all together: "Beware of false prophets," he said, "which come to you in sheep's clothing, but inwardly they are ravening wolves." [164]

The Framers emphasized education as the solution to America's challenges, even for those instances where people willingly undermine the Constitution. Rather than remove constitutional rights that are abused to manipulate the people, Jefferson said the better way is to teach the people the correct principles so they may continue to govern themselves in true liberty. [165]

Of the ravening wolves, Jesus said, "Wherefore by their fruits ye shall know them." [166]

Socialism under all its various names always produces corruption, enslavement, and collapse. Those fatal consequences are splattered across the lives of hundreds of millions around the world. Contrast that with the fruits of the Constitution, a moral code based on Biblical values, and virtue in the people. These have created more peace, economic prosperity, goodwill, and progress than any other form or system or nation ever in the history of the earth. Socialism and communism partake of the grave. Christianity partakes of life. America's liberating light has elevated everyone for the better. By their fruits we know them.

Proverbs 23:7, "As a man thinketh in his heart, so is he"

Moral Code: Virtue is not inherited; it is sought after and embraced.

This verse from Proverbs, "As a man thinketh," is a good summary of the themes Jesus addressed throughout his Sermon. Many of the statements in the Ten Commandments and the Sermon on the Mount directly touch on what percolates in the privacy of the individual's own heart. How a man or a woman thinketh is how they are.

Jesus gave many answers to this very important question about developing a better attitude and spirit among a people. In Matthew 7:1–6, he counseled people to not judge unrighteously, and to not forget their own flaws, the "beam that is in thine own eye."[167]

Matthew 7:21–29, "And the winds blew, and beat upon that house; and it fell not: for it was founded upon a rock."

Moral Code: America's unassailable rock is "the Laws of Nature and of Nature's God."[168]

Jesus closes out his sermon by testifying to the unyielding endurance of God's Law. He likens those choosing to obey God's Law and Natural Law to a man who built his house upon a rock: "Therefore whosoever heareth these sayings of mine, and doeth them, I will liken him unto a wise man, which built his house upon a rock: And the rain descended, and the floods came, and the winds blew, and beat upon that house; and it fell not: for it was founded upon a rock."[169]

The Framers expressed concern that one day the American people would falter in their virtue and morals, so they built protective barriers into the fabric of the Constitution. It is a monument to the Framers' genius that this document has endured the stresses put upon it over the past two centuries—that it continues to forestall what appears to be a worsening condition of cultural self-annihilation.

The Secret Everyone Knows

The secret to saving the Constitution, then, is to become better people and better leaders—everyone learning to be obedient to the natural laws that Moses and Jesus taught.

Without a Bible-based Moral Code, even the world's most perfect constitution will fail. Those who refuse to be governed by these Laws of Nature and of Nature's God shall eventually be ruled by tyrants.[170] That, too, is an immutable law of nature.

CHAPTER 15

Restoring a Universal Moral Code

ome steps to help rebuild and encourage a return to a universal and Bible-based Moral Code are listed below. These are suitable for anyone regardless of culture or religion.

Activities and Goals to Restore the Moral Code

1. Read the Book. There are several variations of the Bible, but on average, the Old and New Testaments are about 1,200 pages total. A daily goal of eight pages a day—that's four sheets of paper printed on both sides—would take about five months to read. If you add to that the underlining of key words to help draw out key points in each verse, it might take longer. Set a goal of six months to finish reading the entire Bible. As you read, list the positive moral codes threading their way through the entire book.

2. Family Night. Pick a night every week and engage your family in planning and wholesome activities. Do it religiously and don't miss a single week. Many families take one hour on Monday nights to review the upcoming week, discuss challenges and goals, and then play games, sing songs, and end with a fun treat.

3. Keep a Personal Journal. At the close of every day, record a highlight or two about current events. Include personal and family progress that was made by living up to various goals and making the traditional Moral Code a regular part of everyday life.

4. Attend Church. Take your children to church, don't send them. Be sure they are getting true religious values, not modernistic debunking.

5. Support Your Church. Pay a tithe or donate funds to keep that institution going. Churches offer social connections and friendships that stabilize the family, and in turn, the society.

6. Be a Parent. Help your children grow by teaching and being an example of a good and decent human being who knows right from wrong. Wise parents let their children play and learn from mistakes and accidents. Parents should not overly protect their children from suffering the consequences of poor judgment or inexperience. That is how children learn.

7. Discipline. Children require a formula of 90% love and 10% discipline. Help them learn our society is just and orderly.

8. Teach Boundaries. Do not fall for the "permissive" school of psychology that says discipline will harm human development. Such thinking produces gang affiliations or other breakdowns and maladjusted personalities who are likely to fall for every "ism" that comes along. A child needs to know that he lives in an orderly world. Discipline is part of it—not extreme harshness, but a reasonable and consistent enforcement of the rules.

9. Improve Your Example. Let your children see that you are interested in civic affairs, that you support your community, its churches, organizations, and that you're concerned with what's going on. From the youngest age, children want to pattern themselves after their parents. Set the right example.

10.   Live in a Clean Mind. Pornography is a $10 billion industry that degrades humans to objects of lust and abuse.[171] Just stop. Every human is an amazing universe of capacity, industry, creativity, love, and companionship, and is therefore deserving of the utmost respect. Those addicted to pornography are able to gain control of him- or herself, even if it takes years of patience. Become self-governed—it shines in a person's eyes. It creates enormous personal strength, respect, confidence, deeply-felt joy, and rich, authentic peace.

11.   Live in a Clean Body. Alcohol and drug abuse is at the ruin of many broken lives, marriages, and organizations. Don't let it take hold, and if it has, stand up against it. Stand up for personal and lawful measures to help better manage this national scourge and addiction.

12.   Learn the *Scout Law*. For decades the Boy Scout's *Scout Law* was drilled into every scout's memory, 12 excellent parts of the Moral Code to teach boys at an early age how to become mature and well-rounded adults: "A scout is trustworthy, loyal, helpful, friendly, courteous, kind, obedient, cheerful, thrifty, brave, clean, and reverent."

13.   Read James Allen's classic book, "As a Man Thinketh." His brief but timeless message on self-mastery is life changing.

14.   Study Judaism, Christianity, communism, and progressivism to a point where you can quickly detect fallacies which some persons in high places disseminate from their pulpits.

15.   Start Reading Again. Religious leaders should develop a Bible-reading congregation. Too many believers have drifted far from this base of common religious self-education, knowledge, and understanding. Make reading the Bible a daily habit.

16.   Daily Action. Make religion a practical, dynamic force in the lives of the people. Read more, pray more, serve more.

17. Resist Atheism. There's a rise in fellowship groups who seek to discredit the Bible and to define God as an imaginary non-reality so as to appear all-inclusive and non-sectarian. For a dozen decades such ideas have proven complete failures and yet they continue to be promulgated in schools, colleges, and the media nationwide.

18. Counterfeits. Be alert to detect those who use Christian names or titles to cover up the fact that they are not Christians at all.

19. Beware of Humanism. Watch for those who would use the principles of peace, brotherhood, tolerance, and Christian charity to obscure the conspiratorial aspects of God-less "peace." The so-called peace of progressivism, communism, and socialism partake of the prison and the grave. Remind professional pacifists who have accepted the paralyzing peace propaganda of the humanists that the same Jesus who taught "love thy enemy"[172] never advocated surrendering to him. The same Jesus who said, "Turn the other cheek"[173] to avoid quarreling and bickering in the ordinary course of life, also said to take a sword to preserve life.[174] The Jesus of Nazareth who cleansed the temple was demonstrating that *Right* deserves to be defended.

20. Promote Personal Responsibility. Be alert to the push by certain analytical psychiatrists to have parents accept their amoral [without true values] philosophy. They declare that those feelings of guilt and a sense of right and wrong cause mental illnesses. This entire concept is being discredited. There is far more positive mental health in the Judaic-Christian concept of resisting temptation and overcoming mistakes than ever emanated from the Freudian couch.[175]

21. Groups. Set up study groups on both youth and adult levels to study the foundations of our Moral Code, and learn the dark works of the enemies destroying our moral culture. Have qualified and well informed people serve as discussion leaders.

22. Support Positive Entertainment. Movies, music, and games that promoted a Bible-based Moral Code were once standard for the industry. However, the descent into raw portrayals of the worst side of humanity has appealed to the prurient interests, and has done irreparable harm to the culture. It's noteworthy that the studios made millions from such blockbusters as "Ben-Hur," "The Ten Commandments," "The Robe," "The Chronicles of Narnia," and Mel Gibson's privately produced masterpiece, "The Passion of the Christ." The growing faith-based movie industry is also strong. In 2006, for example, the Christian drama "Facing the Giants" had a $100,000 budget and earned more than $10 million at the box office. In 2014, "God's Not Dead" had a budget of $2 million and grossed more than $62 million. In 2017, Sam and Keven Sorbo's moving drama "Let There Be Light" earned more than $7 million. Biblical values have served well the entertainment industry in a plethora of delightful, moving, educational, scary, tense, and creative ways for decades.

23. Be More Forgiving. A healthy part of a Bible-based Moral Code is that it encourages people to look for the good in others, even in one's enemies. It's an attitude that smothers hate in the world—across generations, oceans, backyard fences, and even the kitchen table. No one is perfect, but we can all work toward it.

24. A Place for Everyone. For the followers of Islam, Buddhism, Hinduism, deism, atheism, and other faiths, look again at the common value system in the Bible, and see how the free exercise of religion in America encourages and tolerates full practice of all faiths. Americans of all beliefs may safely unite together on living and teaching the universal Moral Code outlined in the Bible.

Review Questions

1. What personal quality was the Apostle Paul teaching to Timothy regarding an individual who can't "rule his own house"? Where in the Sermon on the Mount is this concept reinforced? How does this relate to establishing a free nation?

2. What do you think John Adams meant when he said the Constitution works only "for a moral and religious people"? Why won't it work for any others?

3. Which of the Ten Commandments deal with the treatment of individuals, one to another? Which of the Ten Commandments do you see being violated the most today?

4. Both the Ten Commandments and the Sermon on the Mount condemn adultery and murder as ruinous to liberty. Could such behaviors bring down an entire nation? Explain.

5. Jesus always encouraged behavior among the people that was humble, prayerful, and moral. How does this voluntary refinement make you more free? How does it help America?

6. Can you think of any examples that validate the verse from Proverbs: "As a man thinketh in his heart, so is he"?

7. What did Jesus mean when he said "By their fruits ye shall know them"? Which forms of world government are bearing bitter fruits today? Are America's fruits good or bad? Explain.

8. What is the rock upon which America is built? List some of the storms that are pounding against America's traditional culture. Name five things you can do to bear up under these onslaughts.

STEP 4

RESTORE THE SECOND PILLAR: THE WRITTEN LAW

Read the Declaration, the Constitution, the Bill of Rights.

Commit to memory the five parts of the Declaration.

Commit to memory the names of the Constitution's Seven Articles.

Locate the 27 rights in the Bill of Rights.

Identify specific amendments, bills, and Supreme Court reversals that will keep Americans free.

Preview

In modern business terms, the Declaration of Independence is America's mission statement, and the Constitution is its job description.

Reading these documents can be difficult for a variety of reasons, but whatever excuse Americans give for not reading them can no longer stand.

Reading allows Americans to discover for themselves the limits placed on their leaders. Such knowledge empowers them to expose conspiring, cheating, or over-zealous politicians and compel them into restraint and fairness.

We read, therefore, to stay free.

CHAPTER 16

The Second Pillar: The Written Law

T he second pillar of People's Law is a written set of rules and laws. There are two key points to remember.

First, the governing set of laws for a nation must be acceptable to the people. That means allowing the people time to carefully explore and debate the principles of good government until they can agree on sound and workable rules.[176]

Second, the rules must be physically written. This goes far to eliminate the pitfalls of ambiguous language. It builds confidence in all participants that they are reading and considering the same ideas. A written document firmly establishes the people's original will and intent, thereby serving as an immovable guidepost to which all future generations may turn for clarification.

The Power of Written Rules

Socialism is government force to control and change the people. In the late 1800s an organization promoting socialism called the Fabian Socialists attempted to replace the forms of self-government in England and America with socialism. It wasn't working in America as hoped. In 1895, their official publication lamented,

"England's [unwritten] Constitution readily admits of constant though gradual modification. Our American Constitution does not readily admit of such change. England can thus move into Socialism almost imperceptibly. Our Constitution being largely individualistic must be changed to admit of Socialism, and each change necessitates a political crisis. This means the raising of great new issues ..."[177]

Ramsay MacDonald, a British Fabian socialist who was greatly vexed by the Constitution's "road bloc [sic] to reform," complained in 1898 that "The great bar to progress is the written constitutions, Federal and State, which give ultimate power to a law court."[178]

A written law has served America well in many ways.

Examples of Written Laws in History

In ancient Athens (621 B.C.), most of the common people could not read. Only the aristocratic families had access to the laws, and would arbitrarily modify them for their personal benefit, causing an uproar among the common people. When that uproar became violent and deadly, an aristocratic legislator named Draco was assigned to design a written constitution to stop the abuses and make things fair so that life could be peaceful again.

Draco's laws immediately reduced the feuding, for which he was greatly praised. Why did it work so fast? Because he used the death penalty for offenses as minor as, for example, stealing an apple. When Draco finally died his *draconian* laws were quickly changed.[179]

Anglo-Saxons

The Anglo-Saxons had an orderly legal system that governed much of Great Britain from A.D. 450 to 1066. Their customary laws were so well known that they never bothered putting quill to parchment with the details—these were simply passed along orally from generation to generation.

In the eighth century, King Æthelberht began putting some of them into writing, but it was too little too late. With the violent Norman Conquest in 1066, most of the Anglo-Saxons' cherished rights were scattered and lost in a flood of warfare, conflict, and disruption. It took centuries to regain them.

England's Uncodified Constitution

The British don't have a single comprehensive document that gives structure to how their government works. Theirs is the long accumulation of statutes, common law, judicial decisions, historical documents, treaties, and common practice, all ruled by Parliament. This type of constitution is called "uncodified." [180]

As stated by Jack Straw, a Member of Parliament in 2008, "The constitution of the United Kingdom exists in hearts and minds and habits as much as it does in law." [181]

The Danger of a "Living Constitution"

Britain's Parliament may change the core law at any time by mere will and pleasure. All it takes is a majority vote. It is not bound by the unyielding framework of a written constitution.

No other political body may overrule Parliament's decisions. That is what a "living constitution" looks like—no solid structure, unpredictable over time, and subject to arbitrary change with a simple majority vote by every newly-elected ruling party.

Those in the UK who favor a written constitution say it would help citizens clarify their rights and protect themselves against the state. And, their hodgepodge of freedoms and rights could finally be defended in court.

The People Are Protected by the Written Law

The lessons of written laws in ancient Greece, Rome, and Britain were not lost on the Founding Fathers. John Adams said "No man will contend that a nation can be free that is not governed by fixed laws. All other government than that of permanent known laws is the government of mere will and pleasure, whether it be exercised by one, a few, or many." [182]

Thomas Jefferson said without a written set of rules, we have nothing. "Our peculiar security is in possession of a written Constitution. Let us not make it a blank paper by construction. ... If it is, then we have no Constitution." [183]

In other words, the Constitution must be chiseled in granite, not drawn in sand. The government must not be able to change by whim and will its contract with the people. If the courts alter the Constitution by mere interpretation, or other branches ignore it and don't enforce its permissions and restrictions, then it is as if there is no written Constitution. [184]

Next, *The Founding Fathers' Book of Instructions* points to each of America's founding documents with one important goal:

Just Read It.

CHAPTER 17

Read the Declaration of Independence

he Declaration is easier to digest if the reader knows beforehand its five main sections.

1. Preamble

First, the "Preamble" that begins "When in the course of human events ..." declares it is the people's natural right to change their governments and act independently according to their own free will.

2. Rights

Second, the "Rights" that begins "We hold these truths to be self evident ..." asserts (declares) that all people are endowed with the same unalienable rights, including the right to govern themselves.

3. Indictments, the 27 Charges

Third, the "Indictments" that begin "He has refused his assent to laws ..." is a list of 27 indictments or charges leveled against King George III and his ministers, accusing them of abuse, intrusion, interference, and neglecting the urgent needs of the colonies.

4. Defense

Fourth, the "Defense" that begins, "In every stage of these oppressions we have petitioned for redress ...," has two paragraphs describing the colonists' efforts to resolve their concerns peacefully with King George III.

5. Execution, or putting into effect

Fifth, the "Execution" that begins, "We, therefore, the representatives of the United States of America ..." is the actual declaration of independence. They don't suggest, they don't beg, they don't offer—they state plainly and resolutely that they now stand free and independent. They would, of course, have to defend that position with a long war, but with these words they execute or put into effect their separation from the King, from Britain, and from all their political, economic, and military oppression.

How to Remember the Declaration of Independence

The five parts of the Declaration are easier to recall by remembering to *take pride in America* with the acronym P.R.I.D.E.

> **P** — Preamble, "When in the course ..."
> **R** — Rights, "We hold these truths ..."
> **I** — Indictments, the 27 charges
> **D** — Defense, "... we have petitioned for redress..."
> **E** — Execution or putting into effect

Read the Declaration

Next, take a few minutes and read the Declaration of Independence starting on p. 189, and highlight any important information that is new to you. It takes less than 10 minutes.

CHAPTER 18

Read the U.S. Constitution

t takes less than 30 minutes to read the seven Articles of the Constitution. It is much easier to digest the context and meaning of these statements if the reader first becomes familiar with the Constitution's basic structure.

There are seven major parts called Articles. Each is divided into Sections and Clauses. The Sections are usually numbered but the Clauses are not. People refer to the clauses in the order they appear, for example: Article 1, Section 8, Clause 10. In some books a reference to a Section is made with this symbol: §.

Article I

Who makes the laws? This Article describes Congress's job. It outlines the lawmaking duties of the Senate and the House of Representatives, collectively called Congress. This body is granted 20 powers to manage the nation's resources and defenses.

Article II

Who is the administrator? This describes the management duties of the Executive Branch (the president) to enforce the law.

Article III

Who settles any conflicts? The job description of the Supreme Court and its role as the third branch of government is given here.

Article IV

What about states' rights? This Article tells how to add new states, and what guarantees each state may enjoy under the Constitution.

Article V

How do we change the Constitution? The only authorized amending process is outlined here.

Article VI

Which law is supreme? This Article declares that the Constitution is the supreme law of the land, standing above the state constitutions wherever those duties come in conflict. It also declares that the United States will pay its debts, that office holders must swear by oath or affirmation to be loyal to the Constitution, and that no religious test will be required to hold an office in the United States.

Article VII

The ratification process is described here, explaining what it takes to make the Constitution legally binding on all the states.

Amendments

The first ten amendments are called the Bill of Rights. The remaining 17 amendments are more difficult to understand because they require additional context to see what problems and questions are being resolved. Most printed versions of the Constitution help readers see how Amendments changed the original text by using brackets around the old text, and adding a footnote.

The Real Purpose of Law

A century before the Constitution was formally ratified, the philosopher John Locke explained how the restrictions of law actually allow for broad freedoms inside a land of liberty. In 1689 Locke wrote: "The end of law is not to abolish or restrain, but to preserve and enlarge freedom." [185]

Common sense leads most people to ask how more restrictions could possibly enlarge freedom. But then Locke makes this curious statement: "Where there is no law there is no freedom." How can that be, doesn't this contradict itself?

Locke said the key to real freedom is to pass laws preventing the people from doing harm to others. He explained that true liberty can be present only in a nation where the people are protected from "restraint and violence from others." That state of existence requires laws that are enforced on the most basic levels of society. Locke asked, "Who could be free, when every other man's humour might domineer over him?" The law protects people from "the arbitrary will of another," and allows the citizens to "freely follow his own [actions]." [186]

Said another way, "You're free to swing your fist but you're not at liberty to hit my nose." And that's how the Constitution's framework allows for the drafting of needed laws so freedom can abound. Where there is no law there can be no freedom.

Read the U.S. Constitution

Next, take a few minutes and read the seven Articles of the Constitution starting on p. 195, and highlight any important information that is new to you.

How to Remember the Seven Articles

Is there a convenient way to remember the correct order of the seven Articles and what each of them describes?

In this era of modern pop-culture movies, a whole generation of alien-sounding outer space names have entered, passed, and exited the vernacular.

From Gene Roddenberry's famous Star Trek productions came such names as Spock, Worf, Sarek, Saavik, Q, among others.[187] From George Lucas and Star Wars came Luke Skywalker, Obi-Wan Kenobi, Chewbacca, R2D2, Wookiees, and Jar Jar Binks.[188]

In all of these wonderful and creative names who has ever heard of Lej Sasr?

Probably no one because he is a made-up character to help people remember the seven Articles. Say his name twice a day for a week and it won't be forgotten—L.E.J. S.A.S.R.

L — Legislative Branch, Article I
E — Executive Branch, Article II
J — Judicial Branch, Article III

S — States, Article IV
A — Amendments, Article V
S — Supreme Law, Article VI
R — Ratification, Article VII

L E J   S A S R

CHAPTER 19

Read the Bill of Rights

he first ten Amendments are called the Bill of Rights. They list specific restrictions on the government's involvement in the people's lives so there is no ambiguity should abusive leaders try to create their own list of human rights.

After the Constitution was ratified the states submitted 189 amendments for a Bill of Rights. James Madison boiled these down to 17. Congress approved 12 of them, and the states passed 10.

There are no simple tricks like LEJ SASR to remember the Bill of Rights, but there are many ideas that will help. See *How to Read the Constitution and the Declaration of Independence* by Paul B. Skousen.[189] One tip is to remember the number 27. It happens to fit several things about our founding documents:

- There are 27 protected rights in the Bill of Rights

- There were 27 charges leveled at King George III that are listed in the Declaration of Independence

- There are 27 Amendments made to the Constitution

Next, read the Bill of Rights on p. 209. It takes most people less than five minutes. A list of the 27 protected rights and their corresponding Amendments are in the following table.

The 27 Protected Rights listed by Amendment

I	1.	Right to unhindered Free Exercise of Religion
1	2.	Right to Free Speech
I	3.	Right to Free Press
I	4.	Right to Assemble
I	5.	Right to Petition
II	6.	Right to Bear Arms
III	7.	Right to No Quartering of Troops
IV	8.	Right to be Secure in Persons, Papers, Effects
IV	9.	Right to No Illegal Searches, Seizures
IV	10.	Police Must have Cause to Arrest
V	11.	Criminal Charges must first be Heard by a Grand Jury
V	12.	Right to a Grand Jury Hearing for the military except in a Court Martial
V	13.	Right to No Double Jeopardy
V	14.	Right to No Self-incrimination
V	15.	Right to Due Process of law
V	16.	Right to be Compensated for Private Property Taken
VI	17.	Right to a Speedy Trial
Vi	18.	Right to a Jury Trial
VI	19.	Right to Confront Witnesses
VI	20.	Right to Call Witnesses
VI	21.	Right to a Defense Attorney
VII	22.	Right to a Jury for Cases involving $20 or more
VII	23.	Facts Must Remain Valid on Appeal
VIII	24.	No Excessive Bails or Fines Allowed
VIII	25.	No Cruel or Unusual Punishments Allowed
IX	26.	All Unspecified Rights are the People's
X	27.	All Unspecified Powers are the States' or the People's

CHAPTER 20

Restoring the Authority of the Written Laws

T he Constitution is not at fault for the abuses that have erupted since its ratification. Many of America's problems could have been avoided had the American people adhered to the basic core principles of liberty contained in that document.

Given the realities of today's drift away from integrity and personal responsibility, it is necessary to strengthen the Constitution before conspiring people use it against the American people under the guise of "pursuing a greater good." Repairs must be made in the form of Bills, amendments, and reversals of Supreme Court decisions. (To read the following references in context, see *Constitution* on p. 195):

Saving Article I

How to Save Article I, Section I, Clause I:
"Who makes the laws?"

Power to make laws in the United States was granted to only one body: Congress. It's a responsibility that Congress could not assign or delegate to anyone else—it alone was created for that job.

Unfortunately, Congress violated the Constitution in 1887 by handing to the President the power to regulate industry and commerce through creation of the Interstate Commerce Commission that could issue regulations with the same force of law as those passed by Congress. It was the beginning of the massive regulatory system in operation today (OSHA, EPA, FCC, and so on), now numbering more than 430 departments, agencies and sub-agencies all making laws outside of Congress's official duty.

Solution

Pass a "Restoration of Rights and Boundaries" Amendment that does four things:

1. Strengthens the original Bill of Rights;

2. Restores the genius of a divided, balanced, and limited government;

3. Puts Congress in charge of all regulatory agencies with power to dissolve any agency and return its responsibilities to the states;

4. Tightly restricts the impact of "executive orders" to the Executive Branch only, with clearly-defined boundaries.

This action requires a generation of enlightened Americans who have the ingenuity and grit to chain down the federal government as originally intended.

How to Save Article I, Sections 2, 8, and 9: "How do we pay for the federal government's activities?"

In the early decades, the federal government could fund itself by charging duties, imposts, and excises. Any additional tax had to be the same for every American, rich or poor, young or old.

Unfortunately, subsequent corruption and the centralizing of political power has created an enormous out-of-control central government that is consistently spending far more than it takes in, and is expanding the national debt to levels unheard of—regardless of the political party in control.

At the same time Americans have been misled to believe the federal government's job is to provide universal care and support. This attitude is what makes socialism so enticing. Unless a spirit of independence and self-sufficiency returns, America is lost.

Solution

Several things should be done simultaneously:

1. Pass a "Balanced Budget Amendment" that outlaws the government from going into debt during times of peace.

2. Pass a "Sunset Law" that eliminates every government agency or federal expenditure that is outside the Constitution.

3. Repeal the Sixteenth Amendment and completely abandon all forms of a federal income tax system.

4. Repeal the Federal Reserve Act to put control of America's money and its value back into the hands of Congress where it belongs.

How to Save Article I, Section 3: "How can the states regain sovereignty and control?"

Most Americans don't understand the original power of their senators. These two individuals were meant to come right from the ranks of the state legislatures and go to Washington D.C. armed with intimate knowledge of their state's critical needs and priorities. They represented the rights of the state as a whole, and could stop the federal government from overreach into the state's private territory and responsibilities.

The Senator's role is different from the people's Congressmen. Congressmen are popularly elected and go to Washington D.C. armed with intimate knowledge of what the people's greatest needs and desires are.

Unfortunately, those who didn't like giving the states so much power sought to increase the power of the federal government. The best way to tip those scales was to dilute the Senate as a check and balance on the federal government by removing the state legislatures from that chain of control.

The Seventeenth Amendment did just that. It was passed in 1913, making senators popularly elected by the whole state instead of by the legislature. This turned both the Senate and the House into the same thing: A reflection of the popular will of the people without reference to the sovereign interests of the states.

Solution

1. Repeal the Seventeenth Amendment. This restores state sovereignty so the state legislatures can combat and stop abusive federal overreach.

How to Save Article I, Section 8, Clause 1: "Why is General Welfare costing Americans $200 Trillion?"

The Framers used an introductory term to describe the overall duties of Congress using these words, "The Congress shall have the power ... to provide for the ... general welfare of the United States." For decades there was debate about what "general welfare" really meant in this context. Those who understood the intent said it meant general welfare *only* as specified in the 20 powers granted Congress in Article I, Section 8.

Unfortunately, those who believed it meant a blank check to do whatever Congress decided, finally won. The entire idea of limited government as the Framers had designed it was virtually smashed to pieces. The date was 1936, the case before the Supreme Court was called *United States v. Butler*.

With the Court siding with the "blank check" crowd, Congressional spending and borrowing shot through the roof. In 1936, the federal budget was $6 billion and the national debt was $34 billion. Today, the budget has ballooned to $4 trillion, and the national debt is passing $22 trillion. What is the interest payment on that national debt? About $1 billion *a day*.

Forecasters estimate that at this rate the nation's obligations will exceed $200 trillion over the next 70–100 years.

Solution

1. Pass an Amendment specifically to limit the general welfare clause to the 20 powers listed in Article I, Section 8, as originally intended. Build in the protections needed so these enumerated powers may not be redefined in court to skirt around the intent of the Framers.

2. Act of Congress: Restore the Framers' original meaning of "welfare." Prevent Congress and the Courts from pressuring the states to comply with their out-of-control spending.

3. Prudently phase out entitlement programs (except for veterans) and return the care of those in need to the states and free-market solutions.

The lethal trap of socialism in which America is now ensnared is making the people dependent on the government. Once they partake of government handouts they don't want to give them up.

The European Union is regularly rocked with huge parades of protesters each time a country tries to scale back its massive entitlement spending. In America, voters are no different and generally won't support candidates who want to eliminate entitlements and the numerous free handouts. That's how a nation in socialism governs itself directly into a death spiral toward ashes and the grave. [190]

How to Save Article I, Section 6: "Why does Congress get special privileges?"

A first step that leaders take to remove equality and create castes of "have's" and "have-not's" is to allow the leadership to enjoy perks and privileges above and beyond those held by the people they govern. Congress today enjoys a beginning salary of $174,000, free airport parking, 239 days off from work each year, subsidized health insurance, a rich retirement plan, free taxpayer-funded trips to and from their home states, up to $3.3 million for staff and office expenses, and more.

Solution

> 1. A "Restoration of Equality" bill or Amendment requiring Congress to
> live under the same laws, free market competitions, and regulations as
> does the rest of the country.

As Franklin said, make public office a post of honor, not profit.[191]
In socialism, the leadership always captures perks that others do not
have. Using political power and tax dollars they reward their supporters
and punish the opposition. That is not freedom, that is not liberty, and
that is not the American way. It must be purged from today's cultural
assumption that "winner takes all."

Saving Article II

How to Save Article I, Section 7, Clause 2, and Article II, Section 2: "Can the President make any laws?"

No, neither the President nor anyone else in the Executive Branch may
make laws. The Framers contemplated heavy responsibilities for the
President, but granted him no law-making authority.

As we already pointed out, Congress violated the Constitution in
1887 by putting the newly formed Interstate Commerce Commission
(ICC) under the President. Congress rationalized that a more permanent
group of specialists focusing on commerce could do a better job setting
standards than could short-term members of Congress who come and go.
They unconstitutionally gave those administrative enforcement duties to
the Executive Branch.

The ICC became the template for hundreds of agencies and groups
that would follow over the next century, all making rules and regulations
that carried the force of law, and all under the offices of the Executive
Branch and the President.

In Washington's day there were 350 civilian employees serving a population of 3 million. That's about 1 civil servant for every 8,572 Americans.

In 2017 there were about 2 million civil servants serving 324 million, or about 1 civil servant for every 162 Americans. Why the enormous jump in civil servants?

Aftermath

The tremendous growth of civil servants is largely the result of these hundreds of agencies with law-making powers in the Executive Branch. These responsibilities should never have become federal responsibilities, and those that are constitutional should have remained under Congress where the people's representatives could examine every proposed regulation before it became law.

Solution

1. Pass a bill or amendment to return all regulatory duties to the Legislative branch. Afterward, phase out those regulatory duties that rightly belong to the states, or make them pass muster in the amending process to legally justify their existence.

How to Save Article II, Section I, Clause 2: "Why is the popular election of the President bad for America? Why is the Electoral College good for America?"

Electing the President underwent a great deal of debate and analysis during the Constitutional Convention. The Framers' concern was how a nationwide *popular* election would always allow the larger states to maintain total control over who became President each and every election cycle.

In their effort to make it fair to everyone, they chose a system where each state could have electors, as many as they had congressmen, plus each state could have two votes for their two senators. The equality among votes based on senators is sometimes called the "Senate bump," and it gave the smaller states a slim statistical advantage over the larger states.

While the statistical advantage is slight, it did make the difference in three presidential elections: Hayes over Tilden in 1876, Wilson over Hughes in 1916, Bush over Gore in 2000. In each instance, if the 2-vote "senate bump" advantage had not existed, the losing candidate would have won.[192]

Solution

1. Retain the electoral process as it stands. As the push for popularly-elected presidents grows, the smaller states will feel pressure to help amend the Constitution. If that change happens, the smaller states will become largely ignored by presidential candidates. This is the same argument that was had among the states in 1787. There are today several movements to abolish the electoral process already underway.[193]

Saving Article III

"What if the Supreme Court violates the Constitution?"

The role of the Supreme Court is to adhere to the strict interpretation of the Constitution. If the framework did not clearly and easily apply, an issue was to be left to the states or the people to decide.

Unfortunately, the Supreme and federal courts did not abide by this mandate. Over the decades the court's decisions began to transfer political and economic power away from the states to the federal government. The Framers would have undoubtedly accused the Court of "legislating" in some cases and "amending" the Constitution in others.

Thomas Jefferson saw this coming, warning America that there was no check and balance on the Court in the Constitution.

Solution

Jefferson had several ideas to reign in the Judiciary, including two Amendments.

1. "Judiciary Term Limits" Amendment. Adopt term limits or re-election requirements for federal justices. Life-time tenure for justices made sense in the early years of America. Today, the courts have become so politicized that the mere appointment of a justice has become a political knock down, drag out dog fight for ideological control of the court.

2. "Judiciary Accountability" Amendment. The federal courts have become the agents of change for political progressives who are not able to push their agendas through Congress. When ideologically corrupted justices violate the Constitution, let the states overturn or veto such decisions, and correct, censure, or remove the offending justices with a two-thirds majority vote by the state legislatures.

How to Save Article III, Section 2, Clause 3: "What essential power was stripped from America's juries?"

Up until 1895 the common law jury in America not only had power to "determine the facts," but it also had authority to "determine the law." It could determine what the law meant and whether or not the jury considered it constitutional. The jury could even ignore the law if it felt it would cause an injustice if applied to the case at hand.

It must be understood that a jury could not repeal a law, but if it thought the law was unconstitutional or oppressive in a particular case, the jury could return a verdict of "not guilty" on the basis of their opinion of the law.

Unfortunately, in the 1895 case *Sparf v. U.S.*, this protective duty of "trying the law" was stripped from juries. Judges were given the power to define exactly and precisely what they believed the law to be, and the jury could not. Regardless of how unjust or unconstitutional the jury believed the law to be, it could not "try the law." [194]

Solution

1. Reverse the *Sparf* decision with a Supreme Court reversal, a Congressional Bill, or formal Amendment that restores the common law authority of the jury to try both the facts and the law.

Saving Article IV

How to Save Article IV, and Article I, Section 8, Clause 17: "Why does the Federal Government own so much land?"

All the states are supposed to be treated equally. This remained fairly true until the vast tracts of land in the west that were won from Mexico started entering the union. Instead of letting these states keep most of the land, the federal government kept massive swaths of acreage in violation of the Constitution.

Here is the amount of land in each of the western states still held by the federal government:

Alaska	61%	Montana	30%
Arizona	38%	New Mexico	35%
California	46%	Oregon	53%
Colorado	36%	Utah	65%
Idaho	62%	Washington	29%
Nevada	85%	Wyoming	48%

Compare this to 35 other states, most of them in the east, that average 0.3% to 10% federal land ownership. Such federal control is unconstitutional, tyrannical, and inhibits economic growth.

Solution

1. Pass a "States' Property Rights" Amendment to force the federal government to surrender its vast holdings so they are more closely aligned to percentages that are fair to all the states.

2. Act of Congress: Or, pass a congressional bill to restore equal
sovereignty over state territory to all the states.

Any additional lands the federal government might wish to use
should be leased from the states, but not owned.

How to Save Article IV, Sections 3 & 4, and Article V: "Should large cities be granted statehood?"

When representation of the states was first considered, the smaller
states feared that the larger states would use their strength of numbers
to gradually consolidate all power into their hands. With equal
representation in the Senate, the smaller states felt secure they had a
voice on an equal playing field.

In 1978 an amendment to the Constitution was proposed by
Congress that would allow a city, the District of Columbia, to have
two Senators and one Representative.

Partisan politics was heavily at work on this proposal. Washington
DC residents have consistently cast their electoral votes for the democrat
candidate since they first gained the right in 1964. In the 2016
presidential election, for example, 93 percent of the voters cast ballots
for Hillary Clinton. The 16 states that ratified the 1978 Amendment
had consistently voted for democrat candidates, clearly exposing this
attempt to amend the Constitution as a political power ploy instead of
an organizational refinement to ensure fairness for the entire nation.

The American people rejected the proposed Amendment and with
it the very idea of a city receiving state status so it could have two
Senators. Americans feared that dozens of other large cities such as
New York, Los Angeles, Chicago, Houston, Philadelphia, San Diego,
and so on, would follow suit.

Solution

1. Pass a "Protection of Representation" Amendment or congressional
Bill specifically prohibiting any city, territory, or combination from

receiving the same level of representation as a constitutionally approved and recognized state.

Saving Article V

"Who can change the Constitution?"

The Framers hoped their successors would improve and perpetuate the Constitution, but were concerned their polished formula for a divided, balanced, and limited government could be mutilated by careless, amateur meddling. Madison warned that if amending was quick and easy, "The public decision ... could never be expected to turn on the true merits of the question ... The *passions*, therefore, not the *reason* of the public would sit in judgment." [195]

"How may the states override a power-hungry Congress?"

If Congress ever refuses to consider a needed Amendment—for example, a Balanced Budget Amendment—the states may force such an Amendment into the formal cycle for national consideration whether Congress wants it or not. Here's how that works:

Article V allows a majority of states (two-thirds) to send delegates to a Convention of the States to discuss and pass the proposed Amendment. At this point it is not a legal Amendment, only an officially proposed Amendment. It still must be sent out among the states where three-fourths are needed to ratify the proposed change.

Unfortunately, a full nation-wide Convention of the States has not yet been tried. Whenever the states came close to having enough to convene such a convention, Congress went ahead and took action. Today, some people don't want to try it because they worry such a meeting could be manipulated to dismantle the Constitution.

However, the reality of the situation is as follows:

1. The states will call for a convention that is tightly structured to consider only a specific amendment, nothing else. This would preclude

the risk of a "runaway convention."

2. Anything which the convention did outside of this one legal prerogative is automatically unlawful according to the Constitution—a position easily upheld by the Supreme Court.

3. Whatever the convention passes *must* by law be sent out across the country for consideration by the states. It takes the approval of three-fourths of the states to ratify the proposals. The convention of states cannot, according to Article V, impose something on the whole nation that the people did not have a chance to approve.

There are already a number of amendments pending on the basis of state conventions. One of them is the Balanced Budget Amendment. Another is the School Prayer Amendment.

Solution

1. For the state legislatures, pass a "Bill for Convening the States" or "Rules of Its Proceedings." Stipulate the uniform rules and proceedings. Let the structure first be agreed upon, and then convene in safety.

Saving Article VI

The Finishing Touches

Article VI gave the finishing touches that would make possible America's system of a divided, balanced, and limited government.

First, the Framers wanted to clarify that the new government would honor all debts incurred during the War for Independence. It guaranteed not only the federal debts but the state debts as well.

Second, the Framers wanted to clarify that the federal Constitution, the federal treaties, and the federal laws were supreme over the state constitutions and state laws.

Third, the Framers wanted officeholders to take a sacred oath to uphold the Constitution of the United States. Americans were still learning how to become dual citizens—citizens of their individual states and citizens of the Union. The oath was designed to unify the public servants on both state and the federal level as patrons of the Constitution. Also, religious tests are prohibited.

Saving the Bill of Rights

Two Unique Features

The first unique feature of the Bill of Rights is that it's not a declaration of rights at all. It is a list of preventions against the federal government. "Congress shall make NO law ...."

The second feature is the repeated declaration that the federal government was not to serve as a watchdog over the rights of the people. The Framers wanted that job to belong to the states.

And yet, Congress *has* become the watchdog, and the Supreme Court even more so. How did this happen?

The answer lies in the Fourteenth Amendment.

Saving the Tenth and Fourteenth Amendments: "Who has the power when the Constitution is silent?"

The single most dangerous, damaging, and corrupting change to the Constitution is Section 1 of the Fourteenth Amendment. It essentially repealed the Tenth Amendment and destroyed state sovereignty.

Birthright Citizenship

Section 1 has been used to grant citizenship to any child born in the United States regardless of circumstance. The problem this created is that people can come illegally into the country and stake a legal and constitutional claim here simply by having a child. This was never the intent of the drafters but it was sloppily worded and created confusion. The phrase "...subject to the jurisdiction thereof" is where the problem lies. When people from another country step across the U.S. border and have a baby, under whose jurisdiction is the family? They are not citizens of the United States, so they remain under the jurisdiction of the country from which they came, and so would their child. American law cannot undo another nation's prerogatives of citizenship. [196]

Violating the Tenth Amendment

The Supreme Court uses the following words from the Fourteenth Amendment to take charge of everything: "No State shall make or enforce any law which shall abridge the privileges or immunities of citizens of the United States ... ."

In other words, no state may pass a law that violates a person's "privileges or immunities." And what exactly are those "privileges or immunities"? Are they written down somewhere? Yes, in the Bill of Rights. And who is in charge of dealing with violations and interpretations of the Bill of Rights? The Supreme Court.

The Amendment that those words violate is the Tenth Amendment that says, "The powers not delegated to the United States by the Constitution, nor prohibited by it to the states, are reserved to the states or to the people."

In other words, for anything not listed in the Constitution, the states or the people are in charge.

The Fourteenth Amendment also says no state shall deprive any person of life, liberty, property, nor deny equal protection of the law without Due Process (a trial).

This complex, clever sleight of hand where the Supreme Court has taken charge of the states works like this: If an issue is not dealt with by the Constitution, it is not the Supreme Court's duty but the state's duty to resolve (as stated in the Tenth Amendment). But if the states resolve it in a way the Supreme Court thinks is wrong, the Court can examine it in a trial (using Due Process that is stipulated in the Fourteenth Amendment), and having met that requirement of Due Process, the Court may then declare it in violation of the Bill of Rights, and strike it down.

But if the Bill of Rights is a restriction on the federal government, how can the Court force the states to adopt it as their own standard of behavior? Well, it's easy, by the Fourteenth Amendment—"No state shall make or enforce any law ..."

The Supreme Court uses this around-about process to involve itself in state issues over which it has no constitutional authority, such as prayer and Bible reading in public schools, display of the Ten Commandments in public places, abortion, marriage, and so on. In short, the Supreme Court may use this process to declare the Bill of Rights to be whatever the Supreme Court decides.

Solution

1. Amendment: Restoration of political boundaries of the various branches of government to the sphere granted them by the Constitution. Such an amendment would also return supremacy of the states over issues not specifically addressed in the Constitution as stipulated by the Tenth Amendment, and return to the states all rights usurped by the Supreme Court and federal courts.

2. Repeal or amend Section 1 of the Fourteenth Amendment to remove unconstitutional federal usurpation of states' rights.

3. In Fourteenth Amendment, Section 1, enforce the term "jurisdiction" as it was originally intended, to respect the legal bonds of individuals to their native governments until formal U.S. citizenship is granted:

   a. Grant automatic citizenship to children of former slaves;

   b. Do not grant automatic citizenship to any individual born in the United States whose parents are not U.S. citizens and are still under the jurisdiction of their native land.

CHAPTER 21

Restoring the Written Laws

T he secret to sound government is actually a straight forward concept: Teach the people correct principles and they will govern themselves.[197] Said another way, correct action automatically follows correct understanding.[198] Here are a few ideas to help teach those correct principles.

Activities to Restore the Authority of the Written Laws

1. Personal Study. Read the Constitution and the Declaration of Independence.

2. Personal Study. List from memory the five parts of the Declaration (see p. 89). List from memory the seven Articles in the Constitution in their proper order and recite their primary job description (see Memory Trick on p. 94).

3. Learn the Reasons. Discover the thinking of the Framers by reading both the *Federalist Papers* and the *Debates of the Federal Convention*.

4. History. Read your State Constitution, the Magna Carta, and the Mayflower Compact. Find them on-line.

5. History. Read a good biography of the Founding Fathers, and begin digesting their stories one at a time. Start with George Washington,

James Madison, Thomas Jefferson, Benjamin Franklin, John Adams, Alexander Hamilton.

6. History. Read the landmark speeches and proclamations that formed and shaped America. For example, read Washington's Farewell Address, Lincoln's House Divided Speech (1858), The Emancipation Proclamation (1863), Martin Luther King, Jr.'s "I have a Dream" speech (1963).

7. Find Your Representative. The names and contact information for government leaders are available on-line.

- For your federal senators go to https://www.senate.gov/.

- For your federal representative go to https://www.house.gov/.

- For your governor go to https://www.nga.org/cms/governors/bios.

- For your local state senator go to https://www.congress.gov/state-legislature-websites.

- For your local state representative go to https://www.congress.gov/state-legislature-websites.

- And, most city mayors may be found at https://www.usmayors.org/mayors/.

8. Financial. Send money to groups directly supporting the Constitution, or volunteer your own time to help.

9. Read as a family. Depending on the age, this may vary from simple story-telling to researching current events for some insightful constitutional discussion around the table.

10. Holidays. Observe national events with a family activity. On July

4, read the Declaration aloud, passing a copy around from which all can read. Do the same thing with the Constitution on September 17. Ask the children to search on-line for a brief summary of a Framer's biography and read it aloud together.

11. Birthdays. Celebrate any of the Framers' birthdays with donuts or treats. Figure out how old each one would be if still living today. Share a short biography, and wish that Framer a happy birthday.

12. For older students in school, get acquainted with the Framers and their debates about freedom, to make economics, history, philosophy, political science, sociology and psychology come alive. These are all related to the war for cultural survival in which Americans are now engaged.

13. Education. Students will never have more time to study the Constitution than while in school. Work more closely with them to get a genuine understanding of the founding documents. Help them learn the philosophy, the history, and the lives of those closely involved.

14. School. Be active in PTA. If you are not, progressives and centralized planners will take over.

15. Home Library. Have a "freedom library" in your home. Include good biographies of the founding fathers. Some recommended titles are provided in *Suggested Resources* on p. 219.

16. Study Groups. Organize a family, neighborhood, or church study group to meet in your home or another's. Invite guest speakers. Pick a book and study it together once every week or two. Help your family realize that there is a great struggle going on in the world which they can help to win.

17. Conduct a study course on constitutional or free-market principles at home or work. The Heritage Foundation, Hillsdale College, the National Center for Constitutional Studies (NCCS), and others, can

provide a complete program with speakers, films, tapes, and literature. Many other organizations are also available to help.

18. Media Professionals. Run features on current issues which reflect a solid American interpretation of the problem.

19. Local Media. Seek access to local cable and talk-radio outlets and participate in sharing pro-Constitution messages.

20. Social Media. Use any messaging platforms to share your messages across multiple platforms. You can film yourself with your cell phone and upload your commentary to YouTube for free. If your content draws enough followers, you may even make money from those efforts.

21. Self-publish. Self-publishing a book is now easily done with minimal expense through print on demand services such as CreateSpace, Lightning Source, and others. You can also upload a speech or narration of a book or article to Audible.com and others, or distribute an ebook across multiple providers. These platforms give your message power to travel around the world. See *Ten Secrets to a Best Seller* by Tim McConnehey for steps to get your manuscript published.

22. Start a "Just Read It" campaign to encourage the reading of the Constitution. Ignorance is America's greatest enemy. Solicit donations to distribute copies of the Constitution to everyone possible with the message "Just Read it."

23. In-Class Activities and Exercises: Read the Declaration and Constitution together as a class. Give short open-book quizzes. Include current-events discussion. Talk about how political arguments are inflamed by those seeking to sidestep or violate what the Declaration of Independence and the Constitution say.

24. Define for students the difference between the factors that made Americans the first free people in modern times and the flawed ideas that have destroyed freedom wherever tyranny, or socialism and

communism have taken over.

25. In preparation for presidential elections, instruct students about the electoral process and cite presidential elections where the candidate with the most popular votes did not win (there are five). Teach them how the ingenious electoral process keeps all the states in play, not just the 12–14 largest states that would dominate the outcome of popular elections every time.

Saving, Restoring, and Strengthening the Constitution

Next, *The Founding Fathers' Book of Instructions* teaches how to sustain the material, tangible side of freedom by defending and supporting Economic Liberty.

Review Questions

1. Can you think of three things the government is doing which the Founders would call "unconstitutional"? In what particular areas of liberty and personal freedoms do you feel future generations must make up for lost ground?

2. Why did the Framers believe it was important to have a written Constitution? Does England have a written constitution? Why is a "living constitution" so dangerous?

3. In the Bill of Rights, what does the Ninth Amendment do? The Tenth Amendment? Which rights in the Bill of Rights do you believe are being violated the most? How do we stop that?

4. In Article V (see *Constitution* p. 195), the Framers provided for a Convention of the States to override a stubborn Congress with power to formally propose amendments. How do the Framers' phrases "... for *proposing* amendments ..." and "... *when* ratified by ..." ensure that such a gathering can't become a "runaway convention" that rewrites the Constitution?

5. The authors offer LEJ SASR as a memory device to recall the Articles of the Constitution in their correct order. Using LEJ SASR can you now recite what each Article describes?

6. Why is it dangerous to grant large cities the same power of representation in Congress as that held by a state?

7. If the Electoral College was abolished would presidential elections be more fair or less? Which part of the United States would no longer be important in that political process?

8. What two mechanisms did Jefferson propose to reign in a politicized, biased, or anti-Constitutional Supreme Court?

9. Have you ever read the Declaration of Independence? The Constitution? The Old Testament? The New Testament? How would you answer someone who said reading these source materials is a waste of time?

RESTORE THE THIRD PILLAR: ECONOMIC LIBERTY

Learn the basics of property ownership as a form of liberty.

Learn the basics of the free market as a form of liberty.

Learn to recognize the enemies of economic freedom and how they destroy liberty.

Preview

Liberty is another way of saying control of property.

Every human being owns property, beginning with the body he or she is born with. Controlling that property is nobody else's business but the owner's. To prevent abuse, all property owners must abide by basic rules of honesty and respect.

An elected government is an amplified version of the people's united will. Its most sacred duty is to protect the people's property, and at the same time, leave them alone to control it as they wish. This includes leaving their free market free.

Anything outside of this agreement leads to despotism, and must be refused.

CHAPTER 22

The Third Pillar: Economic Liberty

Economic liberty is the freedom to participate in the public marketplace without disruptive government controls. It is the right to acquire, develop, and dispose of property according to one's own abilities and desires. It is the material means to validate individual liberty.

Economic liberty is founded on private property

Property is *the* defining attribute of existence for every human being. Our first piece of property is the body we're born with. We put that to work to sustain ourselves and produce more property in the form of a paycheck, a commodity, a harvest, a creative work, a needed service, and so forth.

To deny people their property is to deny them their very lives, making them mere slaves, producing for others but not for themselves. Even God sanctioned the ownership of property when he commanded "Thou shalt not steal," and "Thou shalt not covet." [199] Property is the foundation of human joy and prosperity.

It is, therefore, the sacred duty of government to protect human lives and the property they create. As James Madison put it, "Government is instituted to protect property of every sort." [200] It is no more complicated than that.

What are the risks if a government fails to protect property? John Adams said it leads to war:

"The moment the idea is admitted into society that property is not as sacred as the laws of God, and that there is not a force of law and public justice to protect it, anarchy and tyranny commence. Property must be secured or liberty cannot exist."[201]

Those were the conditions under which England's King George III preyed on the American colonists. They refused to see their economic liberties trampled upon and rose up to engage the king in the American War for Independence.

Economic liberty is not merely one of the four main pillars of self-government. It is the power to prosper every tangible and abstract concept and component of individual freedom, liberty, and self-government.

True freedom is economic liberty, and economic liberty is true freedom.

CHAPTER 23

How Do Americans Benefit from Economic Liberty?

The Framers were fascinated with the possibility of setting up a political and social structure based on natural law, but what about economics? Were there natural laws for the marketplace?

At the time of the Framers, an extraordinary book was published just in time to help them understand economics in terms of natural law. The two-volume work by Adam Smith was called "The Wealth of Nations," and was published in 1776. It was just what they needed. Thomas Jefferson said "in political economy I think Smith's *Wealth of Nations* the best book extant [in existence]."[202]

"Wealth of Nations" teaches true economic principles

Adam Smith taught that a free-market economy, also known as free enterprise, will prosper a nation better than any other system. But to stay free the government's role must be very limited.

For example, the government can ensure the market is never dominated by private interests that would use fraud to misrepresent the quality of products being sold or bought. It could prevent the use of illegal force to compel the purchase or sale of products, and prevent the creation of a monopoly to restrain free trade by eliminating competition.

And it could prevent the market from destroying the moral fiber of the nation by commercially exploiting pornography, obscenity, drugs, liquor, prostitution, or commercial gambling.

When kept in balance a free economy will draw out the very best a people can offer. For example:

Specialization—Economic liberty allows each person to be free to do what he or she does best, to specialize.

Wages—Economic liberty tends to increase the wages of workers in relation to prices. It tends to reduce the hours of work necessary to make a living. It tends to increase the workers' share of the national income.

Employment—Economic liberty increases the number of jobs faster than the growth of population.

Self-standing—Economic liberty enables the exchange of goods in a free market environment without governmental interference in either production, prices, or wages.

Responsive—Economic liberty allows the market to provide for the needs of the people according to what they really want, not what the government thinks they want—a concept called the law of supply and demand.

Innovation—Economic liberty is the driving force behind creativity and invention, and the rapid advances in technology, medicine, communications, and transportation.

Competition—Economic liberty allows prices to be regulated naturally, according to the changing demands of the market.

Profits—Economic liberty allows profits to reveal the value of an investment and show if the production of goods or services is working.

Self-adjusting—Economic liberty enables competition to create the incentive to improve quality, increase quantity, and reduce prices.

In short, economic liberty gives people access to the four basic principles of economic freedom taught by Adam Smith: Try, Buy, Sell, and Fail.

1. The Freedom to try—to be curious, inventive, and experimental.

2. The Freedom to buy—to purchase goods instead of making them.

3. The Freedom to sell—to gain a profit from one's own labor.

4. The Freedom to fail—the motivation to keep trying.

Does it work?

Consider the "parable of the ballpoint pen."

This glamorous little piece of writing equipment came on the market at the close of World War II at $12.95 each. In the beginning the sales were relatively few but the profit on each pen was considerable. A Gimbel's Department Store in New York described its $12.50 ballpoint pen as:

"Fantastic ... miraculous fountain pen guaranteed to write for two years without refilling."[203]

Within a couple of years, competition and improved methods of production brought the price down to $4.95. Many people began enjoying the luxury of owning one of these marvelous "two-year, non-refilling pens," and while the profit was less per pen, the accumulated profits skyrocketed. Millions of pens were being purchased while millions in profits were being generated.

The ballpoint pen next came down to $2.95, then $1.98, and eventually it came all the way down to 10 cents. And today, if you know an insurance agent you can get one free.

By the time the inventor of the ballpoint pen died in 1985, the glamorous little piece of writing equipment numbered in the billions and the profits in the hundreds of millions.[204]

As Adam Smith said, a free economy tends to make things abundant and cheap.

Long before the advent of the ballpoint pen—and thousands of other innovations and the businesses and jobs to bring them to market—America's free market system as a whole was dominating the economic world.

By 1905, the United States had become the richest industrial nation in the world. With only five percent of the earth's continental land area and merely six percent of the world's population, the American people were producing more than half of almost everything—clothes, food, houses, transportation, communications, even luxuries.

Such prosperity was a great tribute to the power of capitalism, to the power of the free market, and to the power of true economic principles at work—correctly attributable to the foresight, scholarship, and timeliness of Adam Smith.

CHAPTER 24

How did the Framers Protect Economic Liberty?

o ensure that economic liberty would bless the whole nation, the Framers established constitutional protections for three essential economic rights:

1. The Right to Acquire and Use Property.

The Framers used the words "the means of acquiring," or words similar, to express the idea that class, caste, race, sex, age, or any other differentiation among people would not impair the people's rights to acquire property. Being free to succeed or fail according to one's own work ethics was the very best way for the "have not's" to obtain what the "have's" already had in an honest and fair manner.[205]

Although "the means for acquiring" was guaranteed in a general sense, there was no guarantee anyone would be successful at that. The reason was because of the people's free choice in a free land. James Madison said there is a "diversity in the faculties of men, from which the rights of property originate ... The protection of these faculties is the first object of government."[206]

In other words, every human has different levels of skills, abilities, interests, motivations, and work ethics for acquiring property. The Framers wanted the people to be free, left to their own honest devices, to succeed or fail, as natural law would have it.

To ensure that these "means to acquire" were kept safe, the Framers placed several protections in the Constitution:

Protecting Inventions, Creations, and Intellectual Property: Article 1.8.8 states, "To promote the Progress of Science and useful Arts, by securing for limited Times to Authors and Inventors the exclusive Right to their respective Writings and Discoveries." The words "limited Times" means that patents and copyright protections must eventually expire. This was intentional to encourage new inventions that could blossom out of the original ideas.

Taxes On Property and People: Article 1.2.3 stipulates that taxes must be equal and fair: "...Direct Taxes shall be apportioned among the several states ... according to their respective Numbers."

Article 1.9 says the same care must be taken for taxing the people themselves: "No Capitation, or other direct Taxes shall be laid, unless in Proportion to the Census or Enumeration herein before directed to be taken."

Ownership Across State Lines: Article 4.2.1 ensures that "The Citizens of each State shall be entitled to all Privileges and Immunities of Citizens in the several States"—and that would include honoring titles of property ownership and contracts that were made in other states.

Ownership Must be Protected From Government: From the Fourth Amendment, "The right of the people to be secure in their persons, houses, papers and effects against un-reasonable searches and seizures ...."

Property Owners Must be Compensated: The Fifth Amendment guarantees fair compensation if property is seized, or if an owner is compelled to surrender it: "...Nor shall private property be taken for public use without just compensation." And, if property is taken, the courts must be involved: "...nor be deprived of life, liberty or property, without due process of law."

2. The Right to Sell or Give Away Property.

Ensuring the right to sell or dispose of property as individuals best see fit, the Framers placed these phrases in the Constitution:

Right to Free Exchange: Article 1.9.5 highlights the Framers' insistence that free trade between the states be guaranteed: "No tax or duty shall be laid on articles exported from any state." And in Article 1.10.2, "No state shall ... lay any imposts or duties on imports or exports." There had to be free exchange.

Right to Enter into Enforceable Contracts: Article 1.10.1 made it clear the government would enforce lawful contracts. "No state shall ... [pass any law] impairing the obligation of contracts." Legally binding agreements had to be honored in all the states.

The only exception was for people who had committed no moral transgression but simply couldn't meet an obligation they could file for bankruptcy. Article 1.8.4 gives Congress the power to "establish ... uniform laws on the subject of bankruptcies throughout the United States."

Right to Access Roads and Common Carriers. A critical part of a free market is making it possible for the people to congregate at places of trade or the market square where goods could be bought and sold. In Article IV of the Northwest Ordinance (1787), free access to roads, canals, rivers, and "common highways" was to be unimpeded so the free market could flourish.

Article 1.9.6 said much the same about trade and travel among the states: 'No Preference shall be given by any Regulation of Commerce or Revenue to the Ports of one State over those of another: nor shall

Vessels bound to, or from, one State, be obliged to enter, clear or pay Duties in another."

3. A stable money supply.

The Framers were weary of the American dollar being subjected to manipulation and rumor from outside sources. These caused the dollar's value to rapidly rise and fall. Some people used that fluctuation to their advantage to get out of debts they owed or to manipulate investments so they could become rich.

Congress is responsible

To that end, the Framers gave Congress the power to create and maintain sound, stable money: Article 1.8.5, "The Congress shall have power ... to coin money, regulate the value thereof, and of foreign coins." The mention of "foreign coins" meant Congress was also responsible for ensuring that the dollar's purchasing power remained fixed in relation to foreign money.

That's why gold and silver were so important—those precious metals held their value on the international market and did not fluctuate as wildly as home-grown paper money that was based on nothing more than government promises and trust.

Article 1.10.1 forbids the states from paying off debts with anything other than the universal standard of gold and silver.

Washington counseled the budding young nation that it should start out on the right economic foot: "We should avoid ... the depreciation of our currency; but I conceive this end would be answered, as far as might be necessary, by stipulating that all money payments should be made in gold and silver, being the common medium of commerce among nations." [207]

Economic liberty is protected by law, but to endure the ages, it must also be protected in the human heart with knowledge and understanding.

CHAPTER 25

How Was America's Free Economy Corrupted?

G enerally speaking, there are two basic economic systems in the world: capitalism and socialism. Various forms of each exist in the assorted nations, but overall, capitalism and socialism are about as opposite as any two economic systems can be. Here is a brief side-by-side comparison that helps explain how economic liberty in America eventually became corrupted.

Capitalism versus Socialism

In capitalism, the markets are free of government meddling. People produce products or services they expect will be needed, desired, or welcomed. The sellers look to make a profit by supplying what the people demand. Competition drives the prices down and drives the quality up as providers work for improvements that will draw more buyers to their product.

In socialism, the government is in charge of the market. For right or wrong, it decides what the people will produce, in what quantity, and at what price. There is no competition in socialism because the government owns the means of production and distribution. Without competition there is no incentive to make things better or cheaper. That's why invention, innovation and the passion to develop a new idea has always suffered in socialist societies.

Who owns the property?

In capitalism, the people control the property and enjoy the freedom to use it as they decide. The government owns very little.

In socialism, the government controls the property. The people have very little private property, perhaps that which is required for their basic wants and needs, but the majority is under the control of the government, and is used as it decides.

Who decides how property will be used?

In capitalism, the property owners make all their own decisions. They alone feel the consequences of their choices, and are free to fail if that's what happens. That risk of failure motivates the people to be cautious in their endeavors, to learn from mistakes, to be better next time, to try again, and to try harder.

In socialism, the government decides how property is used. If the government is wrong it does not suffer any consequences. It destroys surplus materials and moves on to the next project, unfazed, unaltered, uncorrected, and unimproved, with no incentive to correct the errors.

Baby steps toward socialism

Examining the complex work to transform a "free-market America" into a "socialist America" over the past 150 years is a discouraging but eye-opening study. Our purpose here is not to look in detail at the reasons America is in trouble, but to look for solutions. To set that stage, these examples of some of the most egregious violations of economic liberty give context to the upcoming suggested changes.

The Supreme Court

The work to socialize the United States has also been driven by rulings of the Supreme Court in violation of natural law, economic liberty, and the Constitution.[208] A few court cases were mentioned earlier. Here are some others:

The 1824 *Gibbons vs. Ogden* case unleashed the power of government to regulate almost anything it wants.

The infamous Butler case of 1936 gave unlimited permission to Congress to spend tax dollars on anything it deemed to be covered under "general welfare."

In the 2005 *Kelo v. City of New London* case, the Court allowed one private person to take another private person's property against his will.

In 2012, the Court said Congress could force Americans to buy health insurance under Congress's power to "lay and collect taxes." Americans who didn't buy insurance were fined.

Abandoning sound money

In 1933, President Franklin D. Roosevelt signed an executive order "forbidding the hoarding of gold coin, gold bullion, and gold certificates." In 1971, President Richard Nixon announced the U.S. would no longer convert dollars to gold at a fixed value.

The Federal Reserve

In 1913, Congress turned its management responsibility to coin money and establish its value to a private central bank and banking system called the Federal Reserve. Since then, every promise the Fed was supposed to fulfill has been broken hundreds of times.[209]

Since the Fed's creation in 1913, the purchasing power of the dollar has declined 95%. Likewise, its manipulation of the money supply has contributed to decades of artificial inflation (rising prices).

Every attempt to perform a full Congressional audit to uncover how these problems were allowed to happen, has been rebuffed at the highest levels of government. Something is seriously wrong and a formal audit would help uncover the problems.

Abandoning sensible lending

Fractional banking is a term that means only a fraction of bank deposits are backed by actual cash. The rest of the deposits are loaned out to people for a profit. That means, for example, ten people may believe they have $1,000 each in the local bank because that's what they deposited. They have a bankbook to prove it.

In reality, only $1,000 sits in the vaults. The other $9,000 has been loaned out and is winning the bank some interest earnings. The risk is if all ten wanted their money back at the same time, the bank couldn't provide it. This is what happened during the Great Depression when everybody ran to pull out their cash, and many banks were forced to close their doors.[210]

Welfare

Entitlements are the biggest and most costly programs in the United States. Offering the needy unrestricted access to federal welfare funds is potentially ruinous to people and to America's economy. Government welfare creates four main problems:

First, long-term welfare support avoids the real problem. People need jobs, not handouts.

Second, it creates dependency. For the most part the unemployed will stay unemployed so long as the money keeps coming.

Third, welfare engenders an attitude of entitlement, of "you owe me," that is self-perpetuating into subsequent generations.

Fourth, welfare ruins initiative in most people, leaving them feeling discouraged, despondent, and worthless.

No one wants to leave the needy hurting for lack of basics, that's why the Framers wanted these issues to be handled on the state level where individual cases may be more judiciously considered.

Benjamin Franklin witnessed the debilitating impact of easy welfare in Europe. It taught him an important lesson: "I am for doing good to the poor, but I differ in opinion of the means. I think the best way of doing good to the poor, is not making them easy in poverty, but leading or driving them out of it. In my youth I traveled much, and I observed in different countries, that the more public provisions were made for the poor, the less they provided for themselves, and of course became poorer. And, on the contrary, the less was done for them, the more they did for themselves, and [they] became richer."[211]

Federal welfare programs cost the American taxpayers more than $1.1 trillion every year, and yet *tens of millions* remain on the government's welfare and food stamp rolls.[212]

Social Security and Medicare

Social Security and Medicare account for 45 percent of federal expenses. Since its inception in 1935, Social Security has taken in about $22 trillion in taxes and interest, and paid out $19 trillion. In 2020, Social Security's total cost will exceed its income, again, forcing it to dip into its reserves. Experts estimate that at its current rate of payouts the Social Security system will run out of money in 2035.[213]

Medicare is in the same sinking boat. Its reserves will be depleted in 2026. The only solutions that America's socialist-minded government has put forward is to raise taxes, cut spending, or borrow more money. A free market solution is never entertained. And that's how socialism destroys.

Organized labor

Trade unions compel a company to meet union demands by threatening to go on strike. In this way unions forcefully take higher wages and benefits from companies while everyone else must rely on economic liberty to drive those compensations. Unions hurt economic liberty.

In 2012 Hostess closed its doors because its unions would not let it trim expenses to stay in business. Some 18,500 jobs were lost.

Detroit was the world's largest car manufacturing center. When overseas competition cut into their profits, the unions would not let the companies trim back their costs to compete. The companies resorted to reducing the quality to keep prices low. The move drove buyers to purchase better-built foreign models—and Detroit died.

In 2001–2011, American Airlines unions were pulling out $800 million more per year than unions in other airlines. Strikes popped up each time the company tried to trim expenses just to stay in business.

With no relief possible, the airline was forced to file for bankruptcy in 2011. For that, the unions sued them.[214]

Excessive regulation and licensing

In 2017, the Federal Trade Commission sent an alert about the harmful effects of excessive licensing. Their report said, in part, that the current high licensing fees have worked to:

- Close the door on job opportunities for people who are ready to work;
- Prevent workers from marketing their skills to employers and consumers;
- Reduce entrepreneurship and business innovation, insulating current service providers from new forms of competition; and
- Stifle price, quality, and service competition among professionals, which hurts all consumers.[215]

Socialism destroys economic liberty

The examples above are but a few instances out of thousands that demonstrate Adam Smith and the Framers' cautions were ignored. Experimenting with socialistic ideas and government meddling in the market place is destroying America's coveted system of economic liberty.

The Answer

To the question of how America's free economy was corrupted, the answer is a spendaholic government trying to fix everything with layers of laws and trillions of dollars instead of letting the people freely govern their own affairs and find solutions according to natural law.

To the question of how Americans can recover their free economy, the answer is to return government to its rightful place.

To the question of how to start this correction, the answer is in a generation of informed, determined, and principled Americans willing to legally, morally, and culturally abide by the principles of limited government as originally established by the Founding Fathers.

CHAPTER 26

The Founding Fathers Speak Against Socialism

he Framers did everything they could to preserve economic liberty, and make socialism, communism and any other "fairness" scheme impossible under the Constitution.

Prevent "Things in Common"

Sam Adams (1768): "The Utopian schemes of leveling and a community of goods, are as visionary and impractical as those ideas which vest all property in the Crown ... [these ideas] are arbitrary, despotic, and in our government, unconstitutional."[216]

Prevent "Redistribution of the Wealth"

Thomas Jefferson (1816): "To take from one, because it is thought his own industry and that of his fathers has acquired too much, in order to spare to others, who, or whose fathers, have not exercised equal industry and skill, is to violate arbitrarily the first principle of association, the guarantee to everyone the free exercise of his industry and the fruits acquired by it."[217]

Prevent Government Control of the People's Property

John Adams (1787): "The moment the idea is admitted into society that property is not as sacred as the laws of God, and that there is not a force of law and public justice to protect it, anarchy and tyranny commence. If 'Thou shalt not covet' and 'Thou shalt not steal' were not commandments of Heaven, they must be made inviolable precepts in every society before it can be civilized or made free."[218]

Preserve the Role of Good Government

Thomas Jefferson (1801): "A wise and frugal government ... shall restrain men from injuring one another, shall leave them otherwise free to regulate their own pursuits of industry and improvement, and shall not take from the mouth of labor the bread it has earned. This is the sum of good government."[219]

Prevent Entitlements and Welfare Programs

Thomas Jefferson (1802): "I predict future happiness for Americans if they can prevent the government from wasting the labors of the people under the pretense of taking care of them."[220]

Thomas Jefferson (1817): "Congress has not unlimited powers to provide for the general welfare, but only those specifically enumerated."[221]

James Madison (1825): "With respect to the words 'general welfare,' I have always regarded them as qualified by the detail of powers connected with them. To take them in a literal and unlimited sense would be a metamorphosis of the Constitution into a character which there is a host of proofs was not contemplated by its creators."[222]

Prevent Special Classes and Castes

James Madison (1794): In 1794, Congress appropriated $15,000 for relief of French refugees coming to America. James Madison objected, saying, "I cannot undertake to lay my finger on that Article of the Constitution which granted a right to Congress of expending, on objects of benevolence, the money of their constituents."[223]

Prevent Government–run Charity

James Madison (1794): "The government of the United States is a definite government, confined to specified objects. It is not like the state governments, whose powers are more general. Charity is no part of the legislative duty of the government."[224]

Prevent Easy Spending of National Treasure

Benjamin Franklin: "When the people find that they can vote themselves money, that will herald the end of the republic."[225]

Prevent Centralizing All of the Political Power

James Madison (1788): "An elective despotism was not the government we fought for; but one in which the powers of government should be so divided and balanced among the several bodies of magistracy as that no one could transcend their legal limits without being effectually checked and restrained by the others."[226]

Preserve the System of Checks and Balances

James Madison (1788): "Wherever the real power in a Government lies, there is the danger of oppression."[227]

Thomas Jefferson (1821): "When all government, domestic and foreign, in little as in great things, shall be drawn to Washington as the center of all power, it will render powerless the checks provided of one government on another and will become as venal and oppressive as the government from which we separated."[228]

Prevent Unchecked Congressional Spending

James Madison (1792): "If Congress can do whatever in their discretion can be done by money, and will promote the general welfare, the government is no longer a limited one possessing enumerated powers, but an indefinite one subject to particular exceptions."[229]

Prevent Creeping Encroachments

James Madison (1788): "There are more instances of the abridgment of the freedom of the people by gradual and silent encroachments of those in power than by violent and sudden usurpations."[230]

Prevent Perpetual Welfare Assistance

Benjamin Franklin (1766): "I am for doing good to the poor, but I differ in opinion of the means. I think the best way of doing good to the poor, is not making them easy in poverty, but leading or driving them out of it."[231] (see quote in context, p. 136)

Prevent Compulsion Through Taxation

Thomas Jefferson (1786): "To compel a man to furnish contributions of money for the propagation of opinions which he disbelieves and abhors, is sinful and tyrannical."[232]

Prevent Civil War to Regain Lost Liberty

John Adams (1775): "A Constitution of Government once changed from Freedom, can never be restored. Liberty, once lost, is lost forever."[233]

Looking forward again

The Framers' message is clear: Don't experiment with any elements of socialism or government forms that would violate the laws and principles of true prosperity. The result of such meddling throughout history can be revealed by sifting through the rubble of former empires that once stood mighty and proud. These crumbled monuments mark the presence of coercion, force, big government, corruption, vice, cultural collapse, and tyranny. So go all nations that recklessly neglect the eternal principles of Economic Liberty.

CHAPTER 27

Restoring Economic Liberty

T he erosion of liberty can be stopped when the nation embraces better economic discipline. The path forward, however, has become extremely complex due to decades of government intrusion into the economic lives of Americans. As a result, most people feel helpless to make positive change, and don't even know where to begin or what to pursue.

The good news is that positive national change can start immediately on both the personal as well as the political level—

First, what can my representatives do?[234]

America's representatives are better suited to deal with the major economic problems with which the nation now contends and it is with them that the burden should lie. It remains important, however, that Americans know what their representatives should be addressing:

1. Transfer all Regulatory Controls back to Congress. By restoring the responsibilities of sound money and all things regulated to the people's house, most unconstitutional activities could be eliminated.

2. Dissolve and liquidate the Federal Reserve banks. Invoke Section 7 of the Federal Reserve Act and return all assets to the U.S. government, and put We the People back in charge.

3. Invoke Section 31 of the Federal Reserve Act (1978 version) and repeal it. Dissolve the Federal Reserve Board of Governors.

4. Stabilize the dollar by returning to the gold standard.

5. Root out Government Favoritism. The term "crony capitalism" addresses immoral and illegal collaboration between business and government to create mutually beneficial arrangements that excludes others. Examples include government bailouts, spending subsidies, tax incentives, stimulus spending, regulatory favoritism (example: the FDA and competing patent holders and the $600 EpiPen), tariffs, quotas, Fannie Mae and Freddie Mac, heavy regulation, heavy corporate taxation, and so forth, all in violation of free market principles.

6. Re-frame the Welfare System. Shift to stronger free-market solutions for employment, insurance coverage, and temporary assistance. Revamp the means to root out the lazy from the truly needy and the temporarily incapacitated.

7. Repeal the Sixteenth Amendment. America's burdensome tax code hinders the nation's engine of prosperity at every level. The Framers designed a system that prevented such interference.

8. Pass a Balanced Budget Amendment.

Next, what can individual Americans do?

Here are some things that people of every financial standing may adopt to restore personal and national economic strength and stability. Stable finances in the home eventually translates into stable finances for the nation and its government. Leaders put into office from a disciplined home will benefit all of America.

1. Track Income and Expenses. It's hard to put your financial house in order if you don't know the life cycle of your household income. Write it down.

2. Get Out of Debt. That means: No more borrowing. Save for large purchases instead of financing them. End superfluous expenses for which money has not been set aside. Build a savings for emergencies.

3. Spend Less Than You Earn. A PEW study in 2017 found that only 46% of Americans make more than they spend each month. The survey suggested the real percentage should be a lot lower than 46%, and that there are many more Americans living paycheck to paycheck.[235]

4. Let Dave Ramsey Help. There are several "get out of debt" programs that effectively help people in financial distress. The authors are personally acquainted with Dave Ramsey and his Financial Peace University. His program uses baby steps to help people escape the debt cycle and get on the path to financial freedom. See www.daveramsey.com

5. Cut up the Credit Cards. Easy credit has put millions of Americans into bondage. According to Experion's annual credit survey, in 2017 the average American had three credit cards and carried a balance of more than $6,300. Total debt that year surpassed $1 trillion, setting a new record.[236] Start by living within your means—and cut up those cards.

6. Use a Debit Card. Pulling money from a checking account with a debit card is like writing checks. It helps people maintain financial discipline.

7. Monthly Budget Review. Sit down the first weekend of each month and review expenses from the prior four weeks. Discuss upcoming expenses and make a plan to address them.

8. Getting an income tax refund? Remember, this is no gift from the government, it's a return of your own money paid in during the previous year. The wise will use it to get out of debt or build up their savings. The foolish will find some way to spend it on a "necessity."

9. Teach Financial Responsibility to Children. Help them learn early how to save half of what they earn. Help them open a savings account. Help them learn the spiritually-enriching value of donating 10 percent to their church or charity.

10. Teach the Principles of the Free Market to Children. Help them understand that free enterprise has produced and distributed more material wealth than any other system yet discovered. Point out that it permits most of our citizens to make a living doing the things they enjoy. In the United States, workers can change jobs if they don't like what they are doing. It is also vital for students to appreciate that the remaining weaknesses in our system are important, but they are minute compared to the monumental problems of the bare-subsistence economies under socialism and communism.

11. Create an Emergency Savings. Put a little money aside with each paycheck and work to build up an emergency fund of $1,000. This is another Dave Ramsey suggestion that really works. When you reach $1,000, try to double it. Use this only for emergencies—transmission goes out, furnace dies, surprise dental crown, and so forth. Fries and a drink is not an emergency.

12. Stop Frequent Eating Out. Fast food is delicious but it also creeps up at the end of the month as a major expense that can run into the hundreds of dollars (and 5 pounds of ugly fat). Resisting the enjoyable break a few times will free up more money to put into emergency savings.

13. Buy Term Insurance and Health Insurance. Being properly insured is a good long-term financial strategy that will pay back important dividends for the unforeseen emergencies.

14. Contribute to a retirement fund. Most employers offer a 401K. For everyone else, get the help of a professional retirement planner.

Consistent contributions, not the interest rates, are the key to long-term financial success.

15. Limit expenses for gifts. Extravagance isn't always the most effective token of love, concern, and caring.

16. Refinance. Sometimes lower interest rates come along and it pays to refinance a mortgage or large loan. Be wary of upfront fees that could offset any savings.

17. Save the Surplus. With every raise, gift, or unexpected addition of money, put a portion or all of it into savings.

18. To Err is Human. Review monthly statements for accuracy. Credit card statements, bank statements, and credit reports should be closely scrutinized each month or quarter. Mistakes do happen. And, fraud can be detected with regular reviews.

19. Set Aside Fun Money. Life should be enjoyed, as should the fruits of one's labors. Moments of good economic discipline will give back decades of joyful economic freedom.

Review Questions

1. Describe Economic Liberty in your own words.

2. How would you answer a person who claims competition is wasteful?

3. What is the primary role of government? What are the legitimate reasons why the government should have some controls over the free market?

4. When King George III abused the property rights of the American colonists, how did they respond? Was that reaction legal and justified? Explain.

5. What does the "freedom to specialize" mean? How is the common cell phone a good example of specialization?

6. What were Adam Smith's four great ideas of economic liberty that must be preserved to make a people prosperous?

7. Do you think it is a good idea to allow patents and copyrights to expire after a few years? Explain.

8. Explain socialism. Explain capitalism.

9. What are some of the policy changes and actions that destabilized the dollar?

10. Americans are a compassionate, empathetic people. Why, then, do you think the Framers insisted that federal-level government welfare was harmful to those in need? Can you think of a few ways the free market could help people get off welfare?

11. If you had no on-going debt except for a house payment, how much cash would be freed up? Would this be enough to cover the expenses you normally put on a credit card? Is becoming debt-free connected to controlling your spending? What, then, needs the most serious attention to enjoy personal economic freedom in your private life?

STEP 6

RESTORE THE FOURTH PILLAR: VIRTUE

❧

Learn the critical role of virtue in self-government.

Learn how to restore virtue on a personal level and on a public level.

Preview

Virtue is having the fortitude to stand up in support of law, justice, and what's right. It is often overlooked in its role as the true engine of lasting liberty.

Standing up means voting, becoming well-read, educated, and knowledgeable. It means being involved with society and government. It means a judicial system that punishes and rewards without bias or prejudice. It means maintaining a well-trained and well-equipped military.

The Framers declared virtue to be inseparably connected with religion, and without its essential role in society, the Constitution would not long stand.

CHAPTER 28

The Fourth Pillar: Virtue

Virtue is a willingness of the people to uphold and obey the written rules. America's Framers used the words *public virtue* to describe such willingness on a national scale. To them virtue meant the strength and resolve to stand up for what was right—a determination to live, obey, defend, and sustain their set of rules from corruption and attack. It meant a free and sincere willingness to sacrifice personal interests for the benefit of the nation. As Lord Acton said, "Liberty is not the power of doing what we like, but the right of being able to do what we ought." [68] That's virtue.

Virtue is Synonymous with Strength

Historian Clinton Rossiter (1917–1970) examined the writings of the Founding Generation to better understand their interpretation of virtue. He reported:

"A thorough check of newspapers and magazines, the chief purveyors of this morality, shows these virtues to have been the most repeatedly discussed: wisdom, justice, temperance, fortitude, industry, frugality, piety, charity, sobriety, sincerity, honesty, simplicity, humility, contentment, love, benevolence, humanity, mercy, patriotism, modesty, patience, and good manners." [69]

Framers were Afraid Virtue was Lacking

Prior to the Declaration of Independence in 1776, the colonies were locked in heated and sometimes violent debates about morality.

The important question of the day was if the people had enough virtue and morality to govern themselves and sustain a war for independence. It was universally acknowledged that corrupt and selfish people could not govern themselves successfully through the horrors and deprivations of war—even for freedom.

The Founders had witnessed firsthand how luxury, position, and vast inherited landholdings had corrupted Europe. The same pattern was developing in America. Frequent warnings poured out from local newspapers, politicians, and preachers that Americans were falling for the European trap, a corruption that John Adams called the "rage for profit and commerce."[70]

Obtain Freedom before People Become Corrupted

Thomas Paine predicted that if the break for independence was not made immediately, that in 50 years the people would be so dependent on profit and commerce they wouldn't have the slightest desire to seek independence. He predicted they would become an extension of the oppressive European elitists and their tyrannical aristocratic establishment of "have's" and "have-not's."[71]

Washington Witnessed Weak National Virtue

General Washington was discouraged by the lack of virtue when he took command of the army in 1775.

He saw soldiers deserting their posts before their contract was up, taking home with them their expensive government-issued rifles.

He saw farmers and suppliers charging the highest possible prices to feed his starving troops.

He saw jealous infighting and lack of financial and material support from the states.

There was nothing reassuring during these war years that led Washington, Madison, Jefferson, Adams, or any of the Framers to believe that Americans had the virtue necessary for self-government.[72] But as the heavy hand of Britain's King George III fell heavier and more ruthlessly, the people grew more resolved to stand up for their rights.

Constitution Compensates for Lack of Virtue

To protect the people from human weakness and corruption, the Framers created a form of government they hoped was immune to tampering. It wasn't perfect but it came very close.

Historian Richard Bushman pointed out that "The Constitution, then, was an effort to compensate for lack of virtue in the American people. It would create a government which in the language of the eighteenth century would 'draw to a point' the virtue of the people. Laws that punished vice and rewarded virtue, that protected the rights of the minority, might prevent freedom from deteriorating."[73]

That's about as far as government can influence its people without becoming tyrannical. As Lord Acton said, "Men cannot be made good by the state, but they can easily be made bad. Morality depends on liberty." In other words, people must be free to choose good or evil, and choosing good has true liberty as its reward.[74]

Only Virtuous People can Enjoy True Liberty

This clarifies Benjamin Franklin's insistence that "only a virtuous people are capable of freedom. As nations become corrupt and vicious, they have more need of masters."[75] If people won't stand up for the right, all else is lost. In the end they will bow to more masters, regulations, laws, and restrictions in order to obtain security.

Richard Henry Lee echoed these sentiments in his 1825 memoir:

"It is certainly true that a popular government cannot flourish without virtue in the people."[76]

Virtue as the Cornerstone of Self-Government

A virtuous people will support the kind of government established by the Constitution because it puts the power in the hands of the people while protecting the rights of everyone. That's why this statement (p. xx) from the preface is as binding as it is indicting:

"We as a people have corrupted ourselves, claiming corruption to be a constitutional right while rejecting the personal responsibilities permanently yoked to each of those constitutional rights."

The loss of virtue is not a consequence of losing liberties, it is the root cause of liberties lost.

Constitution Sustained by Virtuous People and Leaders

The Constitution was constructed on the premise that the people would be honest and kind in their dealings with one another. That meant upholding the law. Without a tyrannical king to enforce obedience, the people had to voluntarily impose self-obedience.

Samuel Adams was grateful that America found its freedom, but he worried about its sustainability down through the years:

"I thank God that I have lived to see my country independent and free. She may long enjoy her independence and freedom if she will. It depends on her virtue."[77]

Virtue is the Foundation of the Constitution

John Adams said pure virtue had to spread among the people or all would be lost: "The only foundation of a free Constitution, is pure Virtue, and if this cannot be inspired into our People, in a greater Measure, than they have it now, they may change their Rulers, and the forms of Government, but they will not obtain a lasting Liberty."[78]

Washington's experiences and study of the issues made it clear to him that the strength of all oppressive forms of government was due in part to lack of virtue in the people. Samuel Williams called this dark power nothing more complicated than raw fear:

"In a despotic government, the only principle by which the tyrant who is to move the whole machine means to regulate and manage the people is fear, by the servile dread of his power. But a free government, which of all others is far the most preferable, cannot be supported without virtue."[79]

Virtue is the Sole Source of "public prosperity and felicity"

Exercising virtue in the privacy of one's own life easily spills over into the public sphere, ultimately contributing to national happiness. Although government should not have the power to force people into happiness—something we call socialism, communism, and tyranny—a well-functioning government based on virtuous principles does promote happiness among the people.

George Washington said true happiness is possible only from living a moral and virtuous life: "[T]here exists in the economy and course of nature, an indissoluble union between virtue and happiness; between duty and advantage; between the genuine maxims of an honest and magnanimous policy, and the solid rewards of public prosperity and felicity."[80]

Virtue Must be Taught

Respect for property, telling the truth, volunteering to serve, apologizing and asking forgiveness, are traits easily taught during a child's developmental years. Being virtuous is one of life's most sincere corrections and grandest improvements. It can't be faked.

George Washington believed there was only one path to teaching virtue: "The best means of forming a manly, virtuous, and happy people will be found in the right education of youth. Without this foundation, every other means, in my opinion, must fail."[81]

Franklin agreed, observing that adults lacking early training are more difficult to reform: "...General virtue is more probably to be expected and obtained from the education of youth, than from the exhortations of adult persons; bad habits and vices of the mind being, like diseases of the body, more easily prevented [in youth] than cured [in adults]."[82]

As Jefferson pointed out, "Virtue is not hereditary."[83] It must be taught by example and education to each rising generation. Modern purveyors of communism like Marx and Engels, Stalin and Lenin, Mao, Castro, and others, knew the power of the family stood between them and ultimate control of a people.

John Adams addressed this directly, pointing to families as the great preserver or destroyer of liberty: "The foundation of national morality must be laid in private families.... How is it possible that children can have any just sense of the sacred obligations of morality or religion if, from their earliest infancy, they learn their mothers live in habitual infidelity to their fathers, and their fathers in as constant infidelity to their mothers?"[84]

Franklin adapted Proverbs 22:6: "Train up a child in the way he should go: and when he is old, he will not depart from it."[85]

He said teaching virtue to the youth is of greater value than riches themselves. "I think with you, that nothing is of more importance for the public weal, than to form and train up youth in wisdom and virtue. Wise and good men are in my opinion, the strength of the state; more so than riches or arms... ."[86]

Religion is the Foundation of Virtue and the Moral Code

It was self-evident to the Framers that religion held intact moral principles, natural law, and a pathway for living virtuous lives.

George Washington expressed his belief that the hand of providence had reached into the affairs of the new nation and lifted it from the failed formulas of the past to become a new beacon of light and hope to the world. But, Washington emphasized, the people must be willing to live worthy of such blessings: "The propitious smiles of Heaven can never be expected on a nation that disregards the eternal rules of order and right, which Heaven itself has ordained."[87]

Thomas Jefferson said true virtue is a universal standard: "Reading, reflection and time have convinced me that the interests of society require the observation of those moral precepts ... in which all religions agree."[88]

What Destroys Virtue?

The most insidious yet alluring tool in socialism is to promise the people something for nothing. Socialists and progressives do this by creating an atmosphere of envy, greed, and entitlement, promising to take from the wealthy "have's" and distribute it to the "have-not's." They enact laws to increase taxes on the rich and middle class and make dependence on the government easy and desirable with food stamps, welfare, and guaranteed monthly income.

Fear Destroys Virtue

Americans afraid for their security and afraid to stand up against those corrupting liberty have no virtue, and enemies to freedom will use this to destroy. Thomas Jefferson said "If we suffer ourselves to be frightened from our post by mere lying, surely the enemy will use that weapon ... The patriot like the Christian, must learn that to bear revilings and persecutions is part of his duty."[89]

Pride Corrupts Virtue

As pointed out by Jesus in his Sermon on the Mount, prideful people are not teachable or humble. In today's modern society, prideful people follow fads instead of principles. They follow after building their own status and vanity to satisfy their own lusts and greed. The better way is showing restraint, delaying gratification, and abiding by true principles. Jesus said that was like building your house upon a rock, which works even if your house is a little shack.

In that dark spirit of corrupted values, judges and political leaders show favoritism in their rulings and actions. When those institutions fail, the people cannot be governed according to law or justice—the legal system becomes a means to retain power instead of enforcing the laws of the land.

Lack of Virtue Leads to Destruction of Family and Culture

Vanity, pride, greed, coveting, violence, and being consumed in passions and appetites, and the destruction of marriage and the family, are some of the ugly fruits of a pleasure-loving culture. The willingness to obey the law is easily corrupted by the love of luxury. This happens when the people value the pleasures of luxury more than the processes that produce the luxury. "So long as I have my house, my car, my smart phone, and a job, I am safe."

Jefferson warned his fellow Virginians that such attitudes lead to the rise of the power-hungry into public office. In 1787 he said, "Dependence begets subservience and venality [being subject to bribery], suffocates the germ of virtue, and prepares fit tools for the designs of ambition."[90]

John Witherspoon said such attitudes will destroy. "Nothing is more certain than that a general profligacy [reckless extravagance] and corruption of manners make a people ripe for destruction. A good form of government may hold the rotten materials together for some time, but beyond a certain pitch, even the best constitution will be ineffectual, and slavery must ensue."[91]

Without Virtue Nothing Else is Secure

James Madison asked in his speech at the Virginia Ratifying Convention in 1788, "Is there no virtue among us? If there be not, we are in a wretched situation. No theoretical checks, no form of government, can render us secure. To suppose that any form of government will secure liberty or happiness without any virtue in the people, is [an imaginary] idea. If there be sufficient virtue and intelligence in the community, it will be exercised in the selection of these men; so that we do not depend upon their virtue, or put confidence in our rulers, but in the people who are to choose them."[92]

Public Virtue Depends on Private Virtue

And finally, John Adams warned in a letter to Mercy Warren, April 16, 1776, that "Public virtue cannot exist in a nation without private [virtue] and public virtue is the only foundation of republics. There must be a positive passion for the public good, the public interest, honor, power and glory, established in the minds of the people, or there can be no republican government, nor any real liberty: and this public passion must be superior to all private passions."[93]

Washington Prays for Virtue in the People

George Washington prayed the people would catch this vision and make virtue a permanent way of living:

"I now make it my earnest prayer, that God would have you, and the State over which you preside, in his holy protection, that he would incline the hearts of the Citizens to cultivate a spirit of subordination and obedience to Government, to entertain a brotherly affection and love for one another, for their fellow Citizens of the United States at large, and particularly for their brethren who have served in the Field, and finally, that he would most graciously be pleased to dispose us all, to do Justice, to love mercy, and to demean ourselves with that Charity, humility and pacific temper of mind, which were the Characteristicks of the Divine Author of our blessed Religion, and without an humble imitation of whose example in these things, we can never hope to be a happy Nation."[94]

Lincoln Pleads for Virtue

There is nothing more important in an American's life than to determine to obey the laws of the United States. In one of Abraham Lincoln's earliest published speeches, at age 28, he stood before a group of young men, just a few weeks after a lawless mob burned to death a black man, and spoke on the importance of virtue in perpetuating the Constitution:

"Let every American, every lover of liberty, every well wisher to his posterity, swear by the blood of the Revolution, never to violate in the least particular, the laws of the country; and never to tolerate their violation by others. As the patriots of seventy-six did to the support of the Declaration of Independence, so to the support of the Constitution and Laws, let every American pledge his life, his property, and his sacred honor;

"—Let every man remember that to violate the law, is to trample on the blood of his father, and to tear the character of his own, and his children's liberty. Let reverence for the laws, be breathed by every American mother, to the lisping babe, that prattles on her lap

"—Let it be taught in schools, in seminaries, and in colleges; let it be written in Primers, spelling books, and in Almanacs;

"—Let it be preached from the pulpit, proclaimed in legislative halls, and enforced in courts of justice. And, in short, let it become the political religion of the nation." [95]

CHAPTER 29

Restoring Virtue

T he Founding Fathers viewed virtue as inner strength to stand up for what is right. This attribute of self-government is the most active of all four pillars. It calls on people to do more than study, think, and argue. It calls on them to take action, to get involved, to live right, and in whatever circumstance people find themselves, to stand up and do what is right.

Activities and Goals to Restore Virtue

1. Current Events. Take a little time each day to keep up with political problems at home and abroad.

2. Be Informed. Subscribe to a good news magazine, newspaper or regularly consult trustworthy news sites. Be cautious about the new national plague oftentimes called "fake news."

3. Where do you get your news? Make a list of your primary sources for news and information and rank their reliability. These may include websites, radio, television, newspapers, magazines, books, blogs, newsletters, friends, or any other source.

4. Read What You Support. Find your political party platform and read it start to finish. Next, read your opposition party's platform.

These readings don't take much time or effort, yet very few will do it. Break the mold and be the first on your block. Look them up on-line. It's part of being informed.

5. Personal Contact with the Process. Most Americans never set foot into their local political party headquarters. Stop by one day. Don't forget to say hello to the opposition party headquarters, not to argue but to hear them explain their position on an issue of mutual concern. Asking for clarity on opposing political viewpoints for the purpose of true understanding is how to help save the Constitution. Become a truly informed voter.

6. Personal Contact with History. Plan to visit a place that is listed as a National Historic Landmark or that is on the National Register of Historic Places. Tour your state capitol building or the U.S. Capitol. Tour a federal facility or military base, where tours are offered. If there's an Air Force base nearby, sometimes there are air shows to enjoy.

7. Others. Service to others is the most exalted form of exercising private and public virtue. Giving voluntary service to someone you know is not too difficult. Giving voluntary service to a stranger is the truest form of unselfish love. That's what makes America work.

8. Dinner Table Talk. Where you have older children, make current events part of the dinner table talk. Be quick to point out anti-liberty bias in the news, TV or radio broadcasts. There is far more of this slanting than most people realize.

9. School Curriculum. Monitor textbooks and curriculum for historical omissions and falsehoods.

10. School Choice. Consult with other concerned parents and explore the idea of attending or forming private schools.

11. Start an on-line school. Develop curriculum with good audio-visual support to encourage learning, understanding and support of the

Constitution, and introduce your ideas to the public forum.

12. Community Concerns. Learn who your local city council members are, pay them a visit, and try to stay aware of local issues.

13. Gain Control. If any of the educational organizations to which you belong are oriented to anti-Constitutional goals and ideas, try to recapture them. Do not try to do it alone. Gather a group of alert, informed teachers around you and move forward as an organized group.

14. Build Your Circle. Get your local Chamber of Commerce or service group behind regular Freedom Forums to help keep the entire community alert. Make sure you attend them, and bring others.

15. On Campus. Organize a student group to study Americanism. Challenge anti-constitutionals on the campus. Publish a paper. Set up a speaker's bureau. Organize forensic debates. Write letters to the school paper. Get experience in making the peaceful democratic processes work.

16. Express Opinions. Write letters, emails, and tweets to newspapers, politicians, and broadcasters. You would be surprised how few people actually take this little step.

17. Elected Positions. Run for the school board and keep an eye open for progressive infiltration.

18. Attend political and policy meetings. That includes meetings for your school, community, political party, or candidates on the campaign trail.

19. Be sure to remain fair and forthright. Never violate personal virtue or values to win a point.

20. Be Involved. Take an active part in the political party of your choice. Watch for the strong anti-Constitutional influences trying to take over the parties. Do not hesitate to throw your financial strength

and your time behind the fight for freedom.

21. Work with Your Service Club. If you belong to a service club, get it in the fight for freedom. Most civic clubs have a special committee to inspire patriotic interests. Invite speakers to keep the business community alert.

22. Civics in the Schools. As a business owner sponsor essay and speech contests in the schools to promote American ideals and resistance to deceptive and anti-Constitution propaganda.

23. Advocate for Reasonable Taxation. Work for a more equitable tax structure which is not arbitrary and confiscatory. Economic freedom is an integral part of political freedom.

24. Do Your Research. Be careful not to contribute to an organization until you know it is a bona fide patriotic group. Unknowingly, some business owners have been financing progressive-front organizations.

25. Stay in Touch. Furnish views and suggestions to your state and federal legislators. A letter to a congressman can carry a big impact.

26. News Media Negativity. Reporters, don't forget hope. For reporters fulfilling the task of exposing crime, corruption and inefficiency in the American culture, be careful not to destroy confidence in American institutions. Negative events in our society are more likely to be "news" than the positive accomplishments. It is easy to over-emphasize the negative side and provide damaging propaganda to anti-Constitutionals.

27. Media. Some members of the news media have the knack of detecting progressive influences in public life and have made excellent contributions by pointing these out. Temporarily, this action may not be popular, but it gives reporters stature as events sustain their analysis. Americans need more analysts who are sensitive to the techniques of subversive outlets preying on the American appetite for news.

Review Questions

1. How would you describe a "virtuous people?" In your own words describe what virtue meant to the Founding Generation. Was private virtue any different from public virtue? Explain.

2. Why was Thomas Paine so worried about Americans not breaking immediately from England's control and influence?

3. What are some of the roles that virtue plays in the formation and perpetuation of a self-governed nation? The Framers insisted that virtue is not an inborn trait but must be taught. How and when should this be done?

4. What important cultural institution lies at the foundation of private and public virtue? Can virtue exist and expand without religion among the people?

5. What destroys virtue?

6. What are the consequences of virtue collapsing? Which parts of society do you think would suffer the most if virtue died?

7. Witherspoon said that even the most perfect constitution can't "hold the rotten material together" for very long. Are rotten materials being held together in the United States today? Is this helping or hurting the people? To where do you see America headed if it remains on its present course?

8. Discuss the steps that you can take to strengthen virtue in your own life. How can you encourage virtue in the lives of others? What can you do today to demonstrate renewed virtue?

STEP 7

JUST START

List the things you are doing to help save the Constitution.

What steps will you take today to "Just Start"?

Preview

Liberty is the fruit of a tree with deep roots in good soil. Though it has long stood these many years, the tree of liberty can die within a single generation from simple neglect or intentional abuse.

Those who planted that tree knew what they were risking, that one day it might fall prey to corruption. The protections they left us are those concepts, principles, and actions briefly summarized in the six steps already presented. The seventh step that must now follow, is ours alone to initiate. It is the most crucial of all. Future generations will know for better or worse if we were valiant to that cause, the cause for which we were born. It is for us to Just Start.

CHAPTER 30

Just Start

T he obscure Quaker Isaac Potts, an otherwise unknown and insignificant figure in history, told of a poignant moment he personally witnessed during the ravages of the early days of America's War for Independence. It was a scene at Valley Forge—amply recreated in paintings, drawings and popular media—of George Washington, the general of the American army, a bowed man whose shoulders carried the burdens of freedom through that grist–mill of defeat and deprivation, dropping to his knees in final desperation to lay his petition for relief before God. Potts saw Washington kneeling in the snow, in private prayer.

Quaker Potts is the sole source of the details of this event, telling it to family and associates, a tale of lasting endurance drawn from the frozen mud of stark discouragement and death among the crumbling huddles of troops who then sustained the cause of freedom that wintry day.

Seldom mentioned about this lowest point of that slogging struggle, is that after his fervent and private communion with his Father in Heaven, General Washington gathered about himself what remained of his faith, his courage, and his inner resolve—and the man stood up.

He stood up against the arrogance of an all-powerful ruler who had dispatched death to smother the embers of freedom.

He stood up against the arbitrary chains of abject obedience forged around the throats of people wanting nothing more than their liberty and their lives.

He stood up against the tyrant who held the executioner's ax that forced Washington and his troops into this forge of the worst kind.

He stood up against an impotent Congress, rendered chaotic and inept to unify the colonies or materially support the war because of their Articles of Confederation.

He stood up against the consuming collapse of a broken heart for the losses of men about him, suffering through starvation, disease, and the cold, leaving nameless bloody tracks in the snow as monuments to their passages through the great struggle for freedom.

He stood up against the fear for his own existence, his neglected labors at Mount Vernon, his Martha, his family, his personal fortune, the things a man labors for to sustain and secure him through such crushing times as these.

He stood up against all that would destroy and enslave and end the great cause that brought them to this place in the snow, this Valley Forge, where the only sentinel preventing an escape was his own personal resolve. And all around him, the powers of the cold, the elements, the collapsing decay of mortality and conflict squeezed away the last drops of ability and hope, and callously poured them into the frozen earth— leaving just threadbare fingers of faith clutched in humble prayer. For this, George Washington stood up this one last time—for his life, for his liberty, and for his sacred honor.

And when he stood up, thousands of others in their rags and pain and illness saw it. Taking courage, they stood up with him.

For two centuries since that wintry day, Americans everywhere have been standing up with George Washington, carrying forward the blessings and benefits of liberty that were given birth by his great and noble act.

Today, all that the Founding Generation worked so hard to give us is now at risk of being lost. This potential catastrophe can be avoided if Americans everywhere will stand up and join Washington in this great work to establish liberty forever by saving our Constitution.

How to Stand with George Washington

This brings to a conclusion *The Founding Fathers' Book of Instructions* with a brief overview of the principles and ideas undergirding sound government.

Along the way several action items were suggested that point the way to stand with George Washington and save the Constitution. That list of seven steps will resonate loudly with the 3–4%.

How do Americans *Just Start*? Let these questions help:

1. **Do I have peace of mind and heart?** Decide which areas in your personal life need attention, repair, and repentance. As John Adams said, our system works *only* "for a moral and religious people."

2. **When was the last time I read a book?** Books are the most efficient form for delivering meaningful and lasting information. Jesus promised his followers who stayed the course, "And ye shall know the truth, and the truth shall make you free" (John 8:32). That's why Americans love to read—to remain free.

3. **Do I set a good example** in my words, vocabulary, actions, ethics, and in my business and private dealings? Do I support institutions that promote the Moral Code, such as churches, private schools, youth organizations, volunteer and civic organizations?

4. **Did I read the Constitution and the Declaration,** or did I skip that part? "Just read it"—and then read those documents again.

5. **Have I ever read a biography of one of the Framers?** Start learning about the people who invented the United States of America.

6. **Can I remember any of the virtue quotes?** Read them again.

7. **Did I actually read** the Ten Commandments and the Sermon on the Mount, or did I skip that part?

8. **Am I taking a little time to teach my family these principles?** True values must be taught at home because it's illegal to teach them in public schools.

9. **Am I deeply in debt, and feel that I can't get out?** True freedom is having the personal fortitude to deny the impulse to buy on credit when there isn't enough cash to pay in full.

10. **Can I explain the difference between freedom and liberty?** Can I recite the seven articles of the Constitution and the five parts of the Declaration? Do I know where to read America's Moral Code? Can I explain why economic liberty succeeds and socialism fails?

11. **Can I explain why** the 16th and 17th Amendments, and Section 1 of the 14th Amendment, are bad for America?

12. **Have I ever expressed my opinion** to my state or federal representatives regarding pending legislation?

13. **Can I think of one person** I could reach out to today who would engage with me in exchanging ideas about saving the Constitution?

14. **Would I be willing to attend a study group** or seminar that would help me learn more about America's freedom formula, its history, and the corruption that now threatens its existence?

15. **Do I believe God's promise that** "By small and simple things are great things brought to pass"?[96] Am I willing to do my small and simple part to help save the Constitution?

A striking difference between the Americans who stood up with Washington 240 years ago, and the Americans of today is hands-on experience with brutal tyranny. The Founding Generation knew clearly what they were fighting for. Americans today are not so sure. They are "more disposed to suffer, while evils are sufferable, than to right themselves by abolishing the Forms to which they are accustomed."[97]

Learn from the Successes of the Past

It has often been said: Those who do not learn from the failures of the past are condemned to repeat them.[98]

But this may also be said: *Those who learn from the successes of the past are empowered to repeat them.*

The loudest and most powerful voices who cast aside America's successes simply because they believe them old fashioned make the most foolish error of all. The very soul of America is indeed quite old, but not because of weakness. It is old because it was founded on correct and eternal doctrines. That's what gives this nation its longevity, its endurance, and its unconquerable old soul.

Every human born, every heart quickened, and every aspiration dreamed of because of the Constitution's promise of liberty, will find fulfillment, peace, and ever–lasting joy by uniting their very best with the living, vibrant soul of the United States of America.

Save the Constitution by First Improving Ourselves

The Constitution will be saved by patriots learning from the successes of America's past and repairing the damage committed against the Constitution's original design and intent. Embracing the four pillars on a personal level is how to get the process underway. And then, armed with knowledge, choice, and passion, the 3–4% can start the ball rolling in whatever capacity they stand.

"What are you doing to save the Constitution?"

In the next chapter are brief personal stories telling how others took steps in recent years to save the Constitution. This is what our Founding Fathers did—took steps into the unknown for a heavenly cause.

Let us take to heart the examples of raw faith and hope in the American dream, and put that sacred promise to the test:

Just start, and the way will be opened.

"Lift Where You Stand"

This short phrase grew out of an event in Darmstadt, Germany, described by Dieter F. Uchtdorf.[237] Several men were trying to move a heavy piano for a musical event. None were professional movers, and the task required both physical strength and careful coordination. There were plenty of ideas but not one of the ideas could keep the piano balanced correctly. They tried rearranging themselves by strength, height, and age, over and over again—nothing worked.

Finally one man spoke up: "Brethren, stand close together and lift where you stand." It seemed too simple. Nevertheless, each lifted where he stood and the piano rose from the ground and moved as if on its own power. They merely needed to stand close together and lift where they stood.

That is how millions of Americans— strangers to each other but blessed with various skills, incomes, and abilities—can stand close together, lift where they stand, and save the Constitution.

CHAPTER 31

"What are You Doing to Save the Constitution?"

I n a national survey conducted in 2017, Americans were asked what they were doing to help save the Constitution. Here's a sampling of their responses:

Grass-Roots Efforts on Personal Time
Judy White, Orem, Utah

"Not having outstanding talents, I have stood for the Constitution by supporting constitutional candidates. Over the years I have made phone calls, passed out fliers in neighborhoods, put signs in our lawn, signed petitions, gotten signatures for referendums, participated in 'Honk and Wave' activities for a candidate, donated to campaigns, passed on information to those on my e-mail address list, attended a few city council meetings and have spoken for a cause. Also, I have written many letters to: editors, the governor, state and federal legislators, mayors and city councilmen, the President, and attended town halls. I voted in every election for the person who upholds the Constitution, and I have spoken out for candidates, Constitutional principles, and good legislative bills, and gone to the Utah legislature, to write and pass notes to the legislators. Also, I have donated to groups who support the Constitution, such as the NRA, Eagle Forum, Tea Party, Hillsdale College, and other groups."

Send Money
Lillie Anne Young, Maui, Hawaii

"We are so busy raising our family and running the business that we haven't had much time to help except to send checks. We try to give financial support to good candidates and to groups working to help our Constitution. If they're a 501c3 we can deduct it."

Read Supreme Court Cases
Luis G., Fort Worth, Texas

"My dad is an attorney and makes me read Supreme Court cases. He shows me where the Court continues to make new laws based on arguments that violated the Constitution but weren't checked by the other branches. Mistake on mistake piles up. I see it happening today."

On-the-Job Acknowledgment
Preston T., San Antonio, Texas

"I drive bus and try to make positive statements to riders wearing pro-America hats or clothing. I post a small American flag by the fan. Nobody complains. I have a group of email friends and we exchange comments on current events to keep each other informed. That helps."

Monday Night with the Founders
Cathy Bradshaw, Chantilly, Virginia

"We were concerned with how America was being presented to our children at school, so we started setting aside every Monday night during dinner to teach them real history. We told stories, we read easy storybooks together, passing the book around. We had them search names online, and read a Founder's biography. The older kids enjoyed finding stats such as how many slaves in Virginia, how many people in the colonies, how many Americans fought in the war, etc. We found on-line games that helped as well. The kids loved permission to be on their phones during dinner, a rule normally strictly enforced!"

Set Up Flags on the Holidays
Steve C. and Dave B., Boise, Idaho

"I'm the scoutmaster for our church's Boy Scout troop. Dave and I raise funds for the troop by soliciting annual dues from families to post the American flag in their front yard on key holidays. The scouts do the work, we drive the trucks. It takes an hour to set up about 90 flags if we hurry, and we typically raise almost $4,000 every year that pays for troop expenses and equipment."

Starting Good Patriotic Habits at a Young Age
Wendy McConnehey, West Jordan, Utah

"We have young children and so any conversations about our country and the Constitution must be very basic and simple. We've been teaching our children to respect the flag and stand for the pledge and national anthem. We also have talked to them in simple terms about respecting others. My husband and I strive to be good examples as well by voting in local and national elections and talking about the experience and candidates during dinner."

Annual BBQ and the Reading of the Declaration
Paul B. Skousen, Salt Lake City

"Every July 4th we gather our family for a nice barbecue, and then just before the fireworks, with root beer floats scooped out, all the grandkids line up by grandpa (me), and take turns reading 1–2 sentences from the Declaration of Independence. It takes about 20 minutes, with me and my wife helping them with the big words. The children love being the center of attention as they take part in the reading. We all sign the back of that Constitution/Declaration booklet, date it, and let the host family keep it as a memento of the fun time we had celebrating our country."

Annual Reading of the Constitution
Kathy Skousen, Salt Lake City

"We celebrate Constitution Day [September 17] by reading the Constitution aloud. It takes us about 30 minutes. We take turns reading one page at a time until we've read all seven articles. Then we take turns reading the individual amendments in the Bill of Rights. We get so involved in talking and sharing that the half-hour reading ends up taking an hour or more. I learn so much every time."

Educate Children Without Revisionist History
Ingelise P., Arizona

"I have made sure my children attend a school where they are not taught revisionist history, and where I am sure they will learn how to understand the principles in the Constitution. Their generation and mine will be the ones to 'hold the Constitution by a thread.' We will preserve it, study it, uphold it, and bring it forward in the next generations for as long as the country shall stand."

Educational Meetings in the Basement
Aaron Crisp, Mount Pleasant, Utah

"I have been hosting folks in my basement for Constitutional seminars ... I've had up to 23 people at a time. I use a laptop for presentation material on my flat screen TV. I don't tweak anything for the non-faith folks ... they are still participating and benefiting by hearing the gospel at the same time they are learning Constitutional principles that span all religions."

Teach with YouTube Videos with Original Music
David Skousen, Orem, Utah

"One day I realized that I had to shape up and ingrain the principles of liberty within my soul before I could help others. While doing so, I produced 17 YouTube movies on "Freedom," and now I'm producing a free Constitution course I hope will reach those who don't like to study—so it will be short. Along with that, I've composed several patriotic songs and written five books on restoring liberty."

Second Amendment: Selling Gun Safes
Jamey S., Payson, Utah

"The Constitution has been the heart and soul and life blood of this country for hundreds of years. Inspired by our Founding Fathers, the Constitution gives us as its beneficiaries the freedom to use the same inspiration of our ancestors to lead lives that are productive and helpful to mankind. But like everything, there is an opposition to the fruits of the Constitution— Freedom and all that is good in the world. The Constitution has done a formidable job of defending those freedoms, but it cannot act alone. We must be vigilant in defending it in our own way. I market for a company that sells gun safes to protect those Constitutional rights, especially the right to bear arms, in protecting and defending our homes, our families and our religious freedoms. It's very fulfilling knowing we are doing our part to help others protect their Constitutional rights today and for the future generations."

Start Private Schools, Study from Scholars
Tyler Heid, Payson, Utah

"Over the past 10 years, I have made it my life's work to do whatever I can to learn about and to fight for our inspired Constitution and for freedom. I've become a student of great men like Ezra Taft Benson and Dr. Cleon Skousen. After teaching high school history, government, and economics for 8 years, I went to law school at BYU to learn more. Today I am working on two huge projects that I believe will be instrumental in saving our Constitution. The first is educating our youth through the Glenn J. Kimber Academy. I have teamed up with Dr. Kimber to bring this amazing school to Payson, Utah. I feel strongly that the youth are key to our efforts to save the Constitution. Additionally, I have teamed up with a group of freedom fighters to teach people about financial freedom. We help people get out of bondage by getting out of debt, making more money, and paying less in taxes. To me, one of the greatest threats to our freedom is our unconstitutional Federal Reserve. People need to understand what it is and how it is destroying our country. I strongly believe that the Constitution will be saved and restored by educating the people."

Start an Internet Radio Show
Stefan Bartelski, Cumming, Georgia

"I came to the U.S. from Europe to live the American Dream and to escape socialism. During my naturalization to full American citizenship I was intrigued by the Founding documents and the history of the American Revolution, resulting in questioning why America was straying so far from the Constitution. Seeing how the Regressives were importing the Euro-socialist nightmare nanny state I became politically active and started an Internet radio show called 'Patriot Come Lately' to warn of the dangers of socialism."

Run for Mayor
Jack D. Monnett, Spring City, Utah

"Several years ago I attempted to get involved in state political efforts. Unfortunately, I found that state machinery was difficult to influence and there was little that I could do to change direction. About five years ago, I came to the realization that the local level was the place of most influence. There are certainly detractors on that level, but generally they are lone voices and can be met head-on without political intrigue. I became the mayor of our small town and, in that position, could work with city agendas and people. As such, we have been able to weigh programs against Constitutional principles and fiscal responsibility."

Radio Talk Show Host
Donna Max, Salt Lake City

"For over 20 years I have used my time as a talk show host on the radio to define and explain the Constitution whenever I had an opportunity to do so. I invited numerous politicians, lecturers and writers to speak on the subject to put added emphasis on the greatest government document ever given by God to a God-fearing righteous nation. I have also incorporated the teachings contained in the Constitution into my Sunday School lessons, which I also gave live, over the air, hoping that more people would understand that its conception and enlightenment came from our Lord."

Present Seminars on the Constitution
Sharon S. Krey, Gig Harbor, Washington

"I've always been interested in the Constitution and freedom, and when my neighbors asked if I'd give a talk on our founding documents, I put together a little presentation. I taught them about the Constitution's structure and content, its history, and its application to current events. I even gave them some handouts I made at home. I spoke about 30 minutes and they loved it! I was asked by others to repeat the presentation, and before I knew it, I was giving my little talk about 30 times a year. I've even been asked to share my presentation at women's political gatherings, and I went on radio a few times. I had no idea there was such a thirst for this wonderful information."

Run for Office, Support Good Groups
Ralph Hughes, Mesa, Arizona

"I have actively supported candidates for elected offices who clearly understood and supported the principles of the U.S. Constitution in the tradition of the Founding Fathers as it was meant to be understood; such candidates as Ron Paul, Chuck Baldwin, Dale Christensen, Scott Bradley, Joe Fabiano, Darrell Castle, newly elected Arizona Rep. Andy Biggs, and even myself when I was an independent write-in candidate for the U.S. House in 2008. Since 2000, I have been active in the John Birch Society, the Arizona and Maricopa County Constitution Parties, and the Constitution in the Classroom program, and two local tea parties while they lasted. I have twice led out in organizing booths/displays for the JBS and the Constitution Party at the 17 September Constitution Day celebration in Gilbert, AZ, and I'm at that again this year. I'm just sorry I cannot do more."

Start a Private School
Dr. Glenn J. Kimber, Cedar City, Utah

"We established Kimber Academy in 2002 to help raise a generation of Americans who were as fully steeped in the religion-based roots of America as was the country's Founding Generation. Our template is to structure the teaching of every school subject in terms of these founding principles and beliefs. The feedback has been tremendous. Parents love this approach. We've organized dozens of schools across the U.S., but more importantly, we've helped hundreds more use our template to start their own schools. It's a long-term investment of love and labor, but a very satisfying journey to help build good citizens to save our culture, save our country, and save our Constitution."

Support Students with Educational Multimedia
Harold D. Skousen, Riverton, Utah

"My father was a prolific defender of freedom and wrote dozens of books and articles on the Constitution, and gave thousands of speeches. About 30 years ago I discovered there were many people who didn't like reading as much as they did watching or listening to my father. With his encouragement, I started producing audio/video versions of his materials, and these recordings started flying off the shelf. When I went online with orders, I was buried with requests. Today I'm converting much of it to downloads instead of physical media. The demand has been encouraging and pleasantly shocking!"

Write a Book on the Electoral College
Gary and Carolyn Alder, Cokeville, Wyoming

"In order to select the very best presidents possible, the Framers created a unique system to nominate the very best candidates. Their original plan as outlined in Article II of the Constitution has been subverted, perverted, obscured, ignored, and discarded by the machinations of party politics. We are so disheartened by this loss of a great idea that we wrote a short book showing the real power of that original ingenious process that has been ignored for more than two centuries. We titled it *The Evolution and Destruction of the Original Electoral College.*"

Write Books on the Constitution and its Enemies
Paul B. Skousen, Salt Lake City

"I wrote a book about socialism in America. I define socialism and show how seven basic elements ever-present in socialistic or communistic societies enslave the people while enriching the elites who are happy to take charge and rule. Socialism is just one name of hundreds that imposed the same disaster ideas for the past 6,000 years, until Americans won their freedom and established the Constitution. I list eight unalienable rights that are regularly violated by the U.S. government to achieve political goals instead of the people's goals. Knowing the tell-tale signs of socialism gives power and direction to individuals seeking to restore constitutional barriers for the restoration of true liberty. The book is called *The Naked Socialist*, and was my effort to help save the Constitution.

"Every semester I ask my college students how many of them have read the Declaration of Independence or the Constitution. Usually there are no hands. Believing people are afraid that reading our founding documents would be too difficult or a waste of time, I wrote *How to Read the Constitution and the Declaration of Independence* to walk anyone through the elegant basics of these two great documents."

Be a Police Officer, Teach Seminars Across the Country
Rick Dalton, Mesa, Arizona

"My 'awakening' to the political and spiritual importance of freedom came as I learned from a patriot named Louis E. Stradling, who taught a 36–hour course on the U.S. Constitution. Since then, my journey has included 20 years as a police officer protecting the rights of the citizens of Mesa, Arizona. After that, I taught American History and Economics for fifteen years at Heritage Academy in Mesa AZ. I occasionally teach an all-day

Saturday seminar on the Constitution for the National Center for Constitutional Studies (NCCS.net), and serve as the Executive VP and Legislative Liaison for the Constitutional Sheriffs and Peace Officers Association (cspoa.org)."

Run for Office
Leonard J Fabiano, Utah

"I bought a few hundred copies of Gary Allen's 1972 book, *None Dare Call It Conspiracy*, that tells about world domination under totalitarian governments. I gave these to everyone I knew to help them learn about the forces working to destroy our Constitution. In 2010 I ran for the Utah U.S. Senate seat against Bob Bennett. As part of my campaign, I purchased 3000 copies of *The 5000 Year Leap*, and we gave them out to every person that wanted a copy. I was convinced that if people had the information in this book they would become better citizens.

"In 2012 I ran for the Congress against Rob Bishop and gave out a few thousand books about constitutional government. In 2015 I started a company named 'All about Freedom' to edit 370 out-of-print books used by our Founding Fathers to get their education about good government. That process has taken 11 people working for two years to complete. The website software is very close to completion now and should be going on line soon. I'm calling it the All About Freedom Library."

Let My Voice Be Heard
Shirley Whitlock, Gilbert, Arizona

Shirley Whitlock passed away in 2017, leaving behind a legacy of seminars, classes, firesides, and volumes of lectures and letters in support of the Constitution, and in opposition to anti-constitutional bills, amendments, and positions by legislative bodies from local to national. She served in numerous leadership positions in national organizations that supported the Constitution. Her strong and consistent support rubbed wrong even some members of her own faith who criticized her devotion to liberty. She shared her letters and lectures with the president of her church who wrote, 'Continue—and ignore the critical remarks by ill-informed members [of our church].' She took the support to heart and carried on until the day she died.

What are you doing to save the Constitution? List your activities and achievements here, and strive to expand your list in the coming week, month, and year. _____

_____

_____

_____

_____

_____

_____

_____

_____

_____

_____

_____

_____

_____

_____

_____

_____

_____

_____

Preview

The text of the Declaration of Independence and the Constitution is copied from transcripts available at the official website of the National Archives at www.archives.gov.

For the convenience of the reader a column of line numbers is printed on the outside margins of the following pages. Readers may use these numbers, along with page numbers, to quickly locate and refer others to specific words or phrases.

THE DECLARATION
OF INDEPENDENCE

IN CONGRESS, July 4, 1776.

The unanimous Declaration
of the thirteen
United States of America

When in the Course of human events, it becomes
necessary for one people to dissolve the political bands
which have connected them with another, and to
assume among the powers of the earth, the separate
and equal station to which the Laws of Nature and of Nature's
God entitle them, a decent respect to the opinions of mankind
requires that they should declare the causes which impel them to
the separation.

We hold these truths to be self-evident, that all men are created equal,
that they are endowed by their Creator with certain unalienable Rights,
that among these are Life, Liberty and the pursuit of Happiness.—
That to secure these rights, Governments are instituted among Men,
deriving their just powers from the consent of the governed, —That
whenever any Form of Government becomes destructive of these ends,
it is the Right of the People to alter or to abolish it, and to institute new
Government, laying its foundation on such principles and organizing
its powers in such form, as to them shall seem most likely to effect their
Safety and Happiness. Prudence, indeed, will dictate that Governments
long established should not be changed for light and transient causes;
and accordingly all experience hath shewn, that mankind are more
disposed to suffer, while evils are sufferable, than to right themselves
by abolishing the forms to which they are accustomed. But when a long

train of abuses and usurpations, pursuing invariably the same Object evinces a design to reduce them under absolute Despotism, it is their right, it is their duty, to throw off such Government, and to provide new Guards for their future security.—Such has been the patient sufferance of these Colonies; and such is now the necessity which constrains them to alter their former Systems of Government. The history of the present King of Great Britain is a history of repeated injuries and usurpations, all having in direct object the establishment of an absolute Tyranny over these States. To prove this, let Facts be submitted to a candid world.

HE has refused his Assent to Laws, the most wholesome and necessary for the public good.

HE has forbidden his Governors to pass Laws of immediate and pressing importance, unless suspended in their operation till his Assent should be obtained; and when so suspended, he has utterly neglected to attend to them.

HE has refused to pass other Laws for the accommodation of large districts of people, unless those people would relinquish the right of Representation in the Legislature, a right inestimable to them and formidable to tyrants only.

HE has called together legislative bodies at places unusual, uncomfortable, and distant from the depository of their public Records, for the sole purpose of fatiguing them into compliance with his measures.

HE has dissolved Representative Houses repeatedly, for opposing with manly firmness his invasions on the rights of the people.

HE has refused for a long time, after such dissolutions, to cause others to be elected; whereby the Legislative powers, incapable of Annihilation, have returned to the People at large for their exercise; the State remaining in the mean time exposed to all the dangers of invasion from without, and convulsions within.

HE has endeavoured to prevent the population of these States; for that purpose obstructing the Laws for Naturalization of Foreigners;

refusing to pass others to encourage their migrations hither, and raising the conditions of new Appropriations of Lands.

HE has obstructed the Administration of Justice, by refusing his Assent to Laws for establishing Judiciary powers.

HE has made Judges dependent on his Will alone, for the tenure of their offices, and the amount and payment of their salaries.

HE has erected a multitude of New Offices, and sent hither swarms of Officers to harass our people, and eat out their substance.

HE has kept among us, in times of peace, Standing Armies without the Consent of our legislatures.

HE has affected to render the Military independent of and superior to the Civil power.

HE has combined with others to subject us to a jurisdiction foreign to our constitution, and unacknowledged by our laws; giving his Assent to their Acts of pretended Legislation:

FOR Quartering large bodies of armed troops among us:

FOR protecting them, by a mock Trial, from punishment for any Murders which they should commit on the Inhabitants of these States:

FOR cutting off our Trade with all parts of the world:

FOR imposing Taxes on us without our Consent:

FOR depriving us in many cases, of the benefits of Trial by Jury:

FOR transporting us beyond Seas to be tried for pretended offences:

FOR abolishing the free System of English Laws in a neighboring Province, establishing therein an Arbitrary government, and enlarging its Boundaries so as to render it at once an example and fit instrument for introducing the same absolute rule into these Colonies:

FOR taking away our Charters, abolishing our most valuable Laws, and altering fundamentally the Forms of our Governments:

FOR suspending our own Legislatures, and declaring themselves invested with power to legislate for us in all cases whatsoever.

HE has abdicated Government here, by declaring us out of his Protection and waging War against us.

HE has plundered our seas, ravaged our Coasts, burnt our towns, and destroyed the lives of our people.

HE is at this time transporting large Armies of foreign Mercenaries to compleat the works of death, desolation and tyranny, already begun with circumstances of Cruelty & perfidy scarcely paralleled in the most barbarous ages, and totally unworthy the Head of a civilized nation.

HE has constrained our fellow Citizens taken Captive on the high Seas to bear Arms against their Country, to become the executioners of their friends and Brethren, or to fall themselves by their Hands.

HE has excited domestic insurrections amongst us, and has endeavoured to bring on the inhabitants of our frontiers, the merciless Indian Savages, whose known rule of warfare, is an undistinguished destruction of all ages, sexes and conditions.

IN every stage of these Oppressions We have Petitioned for Redress in the most humble terms: Our repeated Petitions have been answered only by repeated injury. A Prince whose character is thus marked by every act which may define a Tyrant, is unfit to be the ruler of a free people.

NOR have We been wanting in attentions to our British brethren. We have warned them from time to time of attempts by their legislature to extend an unwarrantable jurisdiction over us. We have reminded them of the circumstances of our emigration and settlement here. We have appealed to their native justice and magnanimity, and we have conjured them by the ties of our common kindred to disavow these usurpations, which, would inevitably interrupt our connections and correspondence. They too have been deaf to the voice of justice and of consanguinity. We must, therefore, acquiesce in the necessity, which denounces our Separation, and hold them, as we hold the rest of mankind, Enemies in War, in Peace Friends.

WE, therefore, the Representatives of the UNITED STATES OF AMERICA, in General Congress, Assembled, appealing to the Supreme Judge of the world for the rectitude of our intentions, do, in the Name, and by Authority of the good People of these Colonies, solemnly publish and declare, That these United Colonies are, and of Right ought to be

Free and Independent States; that they are Absolved from all Allegiance
to the British Crown, and that all political connection between them
and the State of Great Britain, is and ought to be totally dissolved; and
that as Free and Independent States, they have full Power to levy War,
conclude Peace, contract Alliances, establish Commerce, and to do all
other Acts and Things which Independent States may of right do. And
for the support of this Declaration, with a firm reliance on the protection
of divine Providence, we mutually pledge to each other our Lives, our
Fortunes and our sacred Honor.

THE CONSTITUTION
OF THE UNITED STATES

Signed 1787, Ratified 1789

W e the People of the United States, in Order to form a
more perfect Union, establish Justice, insure domestic
Tranquility, provide for the common defence, promote
the general Welfare, and secure the Blessings of Liberty
to ourselves and our Posterity, do ordain and establish this Constitution for the United States of America.

Article I.

SECTION 1. All legislative Powers herein granted shall be vested
in a Congress of the United States, which shall consist of a Senate
and House of Representatives.

SECTION 2. The House of Representatives shall be composed
of Members chosen every second Year by the People of the several
States, and the Electors in each State shall have the Qualifications
requisite for Electors of the most numerous Branch of the State
Legislature.

No Person shall be a Representative who shall not have attained
to the Age of twenty five Years, and been seven Years a Citizen of the
United States, and who shall not, when elected, be an Inhabitant of
that State in which he shall be chosen.

[Representatives and direct Taxes shall be apportioned among the
several States which may be included within this Union, according to
their respective Numbers, which shall be determined by adding to the
whole Number of free Persons, including those bound to Service for
a Term of Years, and excluding Indians not taxed, three fifths of all

other Persons.][1] The actual Enumeration shall be made within three Years after the first Meeting of the Congress of the United States, and within every subsequent Term of ten Years, in such Manner as they shall by Law direct. The Number of Representatives shall not exceed one for every thirty Thousand, but each State shall have at Least one Representative; and until such enumeration shall be made, the State of New Hampshire shall be entitled to choose three, Massachusetts eight, Rhode Island and Providence Plantations one, Connecticut five, New York six, New Jersey four, Pennsylvania eight, Delaware one, Maryland six, Virginia ten, North Carolina five, South Carolina five and Georgia three.

When vacancies happen in the Representation from any State, the Executive Authority thereof shall issue Writs of Election to fill such Vacancies.

The House of Representatives shall choose their Speaker and other Officers; and shall have the sole Power of Impeachment.

SECTION 3. The Senate of the United States shall be composed of two Senators from each State, [chosen by the Legislature thereof,][2] for six Years; and each Senator shall have one Vote.

Immediately after they shall be assembled in Consequence of the first Election, they shall be divided as equally as may be into three Classes. The Seats of the Senators of the first Class shall be vacated at the Expiration of the second Year, of the second Class at the Expiration of the fourth Year, and of the third Class at the Expiration of the sixth Year, so that one third may be chosen every second Year; [and if Vacancies happen by Resignation, or otherwise, during the Recess of the Legislature of any State, the Executive thereof may make temporary Appointments until the next Meeting of the Legislature, which shall then fill such Vacancies.][3] No person shall be a Senator who shall not have attained to the Age of thirty Years, and been nine Years a Citizen

---

1   Changed by section 2 of the Fourteenth Amendment.
2   Changed by the Seventeenth Amendment.
3   Also changed by the Seventeenth Amendment.

of the United States, and who shall not, when elected, be an Inhabitant of that State for which he shall be chosen.

The Vice President of the United States shall be President of the Senate, but shall have no Vote, unless they be equally divided.

The Senate shall choose their other Officers, and also a President pro tempore, in the absence of the Vice President, or when he shall exercise the Office of President of the United States.

The Senate shall have the sole Power to try all Impeachments. When sitting for that Purpose, they shall be on Oath or Affirmation. When the President of the United States is tried, the Chief Justice shall preside: And no Person shall be convicted without the Concurrence of two thirds of the Members present.

Judgment in Cases of Impeachment shall not extend further than to removal from Office, and disqualification to hold and enjoy any Office of honor, Trust or Profit under the United States: but the Party convicted shall nevertheless be liable and subject to Indictment, Trial, Judgment and Punishment, according to Law.

SECTION 4. The Times, Places and Manner of holding Elections for Senators and Representatives, shall be prescribed in each State by the Legislature thereof; but the Congress may at any time by Law make or alter such Regulations, except as to the Place of Choosing Senators.

The Congress shall assemble at least once in every Year, and such Meeting shall be [on the first Monday in December,][4] unless they shall by Law appoint a different Day.

SECTION 5. Each House shall be the Judge of the Elections, Returns and Qualifications of its own Members, and a Majority of each shall constitute a Quorum to do Business; but a smaller number may adjourn from day to day, and may be authorized to compel the Attendance of absent Members, in such Manner, and under such Penalties as each House may provide.

---

4   Changed by section 2 of the Twentieth Amendment.

Each House may determine the Rules of its Proceedings, punish its Members for disorderly Behavior, and, with the Concurrence of two-thirds, expel a Member.

Each House shall keep a Journal of its Proceedings, and from time to time publish the same, excepting such Parts as may in their Judgment require Secrecy; and the Yeas and Nays of the Members of either House on any question shall, at the Desire of one fifth of those Present, be entered on the Journal.

Neither House, during the Session of Congress, shall, without the Consent of the other, adjourn for more than three days, nor to any other Place than that in which the two Houses shall be sitting.

SECTION 6. The Senators and Representatives shall receive a Compensation for their Services, to be ascertained by Law, and paid out of the Treasury of the United States. They shall in all Cases, except Treason, Felony and Breach of the Peace, be privileged from Arrest during their Attendance at the Session of their respective Houses, and in going to and returning from the same; and for any Speech or Debate in either House, they shall not be questioned in any other Place.

No Senator or Representative shall, during the Time for which he was elected, be appointed to any civil Office under the Authority of the United States which shall have been created, or the Emoluments whereof shall have been increased during such time; and no Person holding any Office under the United States, shall be a Member of either House during his Continuance in Office.

SECTION 7. All bills for raising Revenue shall originate in the House of Representatives; but the Senate may propose or concur with Amendments as on other Bills.

Every Bill which shall have passed the House of Representatives and the Senate, shall, before it become a Law, be presented to the President of the United States; If he approve he shall sign it, but if

not he shall return it, with his Objections to that House in which it
shall have originated, who shall enter the Objections at large on their
Journal, and proceed to reconsider it. If after such Reconsideration two
thirds of that House shall agree to pass the Bill, it shall be sent, together
with the Objections, to the other House, by which it shall likewise
be reconsidered, and if approved by two thirds of that House, it shall
become a Law. But in all such Cases the Votes of both Houses shall be
determined by Yeas and Nays, and the Names of the Persons voting
for and against the Bill shall be entered on the Journal of each House
respectively. If any Bill shall not be returned by the President within
ten Days (Sundays excepted) after it shall have been presented to him,
the Same shall be a Law, in like Manner as if he had signed it, unless
the Congress by their Adjournment prevent its Return, in which Case
it shall not be a Law.

Every Order, Resolution, or Vote to which the Concurrence of the
Senate and House of Representatives may be necessary (except on a
question of Adjournment) shall be presented to the President of the
United States; and before the Same shall take Effect, shall be approved
by him, or being disapproved by him, shall be repassed by two thirds
of the Senate and House of Representatives, according to the Rules and
Limitations prescribed in the Case of a Bill.

SECTION 8. The Congress shall have Power To lay and collect
Taxes, Duties, Imposts and Excises, to pay the Debts and provide
for the common Defence and general Welfare of the United States;
but all Duties, Imposts and Excises shall be uniform throughout
the United States;

To borrow money on the credit of the United States;

To regulate Commerce with foreign Nations, and among the several
States, and with the Indian Tribes;

To establish an uniform Rule of Naturalization, and uniform Laws
on the subject of Bankruptcies throughout the United States;

To coin Money, regulate the Value thereof, and of foreign Coin, and fix the Standard of Weights and Measures;

To provide for the Punishment of counterfeiting the Securities and current Coin of the United States;

To establish Post Offices and Post Roads;

To promote the Progress of Science and useful Arts, by securing for limited Times to Authors and Inventors the exclusive Right to their respective Writings and Discoveries;

To constitute Tribunals inferior to the supreme Court;

To define and punish Piracies and Felonies committed on the high Seas, and Offenses against the Law of Nations;

To declare War, grant Letters of Marque and Reprisal, and make Rules concerning Captures on Land and Water;

To raise and support Armies, but no Appropriation of Money to that Use shall be for a longer Term than two Years;

To provide and maintain a Navy;

To make Rules for the Government and Regulation of the land and naval Forces;

To provide for calling forth the Militia to execute the Laws of the Union, suppress Insurrections and repel Invasions;

To provide for organizing, arming, and disciplining, the Militia, and for governing such Part of them as may be employed in the Service of the United States, reserving to the States respectively, the Appointment of the Officers, and the Authority of training the Militia according to the discipline prescribed by Congress;

To exercise exclusive Legislation in all Cases whatsoever, over such District (not exceeding ten Miles square) as may, by Cession of particular States, and the acceptance of Congress, become the Seat of the Government of the United States, and to exercise like Authority over all Places purchased by the Consent of the Legislature of the State in which the Same shall be, for the Erection of Forts, Magazines, Arsenals, dock-Yards, and other needful Buildings; And To make all Laws which shall be necessary and proper for carrying into Execution the foregoing Powers, and all other Powers vested by this Constitution in the Government of the United States, or in any Department or Officer thereof.

SECTION 9. The Migration or Importation of such Persons as any of the States now existing shall think proper to admit, shall not be prohibited by the Congress prior to the Year one thousand eight hundred and eight, but a tax or duty may be imposed on such Importation, not exceeding ten dollars for each Person.

The privilege of the Writ of Habeas Corpus shall not be suspended, unless when in Cases of Rebellion or Invasion the public Safety may require it.

No Bill of Attainder or ex post facto Law shall be passed.

No capitation, or other direct, Tax shall be laid, unless in Proportion to the Census or Enumeration here in before directed to be taken.[5]

No Tax or Duty shall be laid on Articles exported from any State.

No Preference shall be given by any Regulation of Commerce or Revenue to the Ports of one State over those of another: nor shall Vessels bound to, or from, one State, be obliged to enter, clear, or pay Duties in another.

No Money shall be drawn from the Treasury, but in Consequence of Appropriations made by Law; and a regular Statement and Account of the Receipts and Expenditures of all public Money shall be published from time to time.

No Title of Nobility shall be granted by the United States: And no Person holding any Office of Profit or Trust under them, shall, without the Consent of the Congress, accept of any present, Emolument, Office, or Title, of any kind whatever, from any King, Prince or foreign State.

SECTION 10. No State shall enter into any Treaty, Alliance, or Confederation; grant Letters of Marque and Reprisal; coin Money; emit Bills of Credit; make any Thing but gold and silver Coin a Tender in Payment of Debts; pass any Bill of Attainder, ex post facto Law, or Law impairing the Obligation of Contracts, or

---

5   See Sixteenth Amendment.

grant any Title of Nobility.

No State shall, without the Consent of the Congress, lay any Imposts or Duties on Imports or Exports, except what may be absolutely necessary for executing its inspection Laws: and the net Produce of all Duties and Imposts, laid by any State on Imports or Exports, shall be for the Use of the Treasury of the United States; and all such Laws shall be subject to the Revision and Control of the Congress.

No State shall, without the Consent of Congress, lay any duty of Tonnage, keep Troops, or Ships of War in time of Peace, enter into any Agreement or Compact with another State, or with a foreign Power, or engage in War, unless actually invaded, or in such imminent Danger as will not admit of delay.

Article II.

SECTION 1. The executive Power shall be vested in a President of the United States of America. He shall hold his Office during the Term of four Years, and, together with the Vice-President chosen for the same Term, be elected, as follows:

Each State shall appoint, in such Manner as the Legislature thereof may direct, a Number of Electors, equal to the whole Number of Senators and Representatives to which the State may be entitled in the Congress: but no Senator or Representative, or Person holding an Office of Trust or Profit under the United States, shall be appointed an Elector.

[The Electors shall meet in their respective States, and vote by Ballot for two persons, of whom one at least shall not lie an Inhabitant of the same State with themselves. And they shall make a List of all the Persons voted for, and of the Number of Votes for each; which List they shall sign and certify, and transmit sealed to the Seat of the Government of the United States, directed to the President of the Senate. The President of the Senate shall, in the Presence of the Senate and House of Representatives, open all the Certificates, and the Votes

shall then be counted. The Person having the greatest Number of Votes
shall be the President, if such Number be a Majority of the whole
Number of Electors appointed; and if there be more than one who have
such Majority, and have an equal Number of Votes, then the House
of Representatives shall immediately choose by Ballot one of them for
President; and if no Person have a Majority, then from the five highest
on the List the said House shall in like Manner choose the President.
But in choosing the President, the Votes shall be taken by States, the
Representation from each State having one Vote; a quorum for this
Purpose shall consist of a Member or Members from two-thirds of the
States, and a Majority of all the States shall be necessary to a Choice.
In every Case, after the Choice of the President, the Person having the
greatest Number of Votes of the Electors shall be the Vice President.
But if there should remain two or more who have equal Votes, the
Senate shall choose from them by Ballot the Vice-President.][6]

The Congress may determine the Time of choosing the Electors,
and the Day on which they shall give their Votes; which Day shall be
the same throughout the United States.

No person except a natural born Citizen, or a Citizen of the United
States, at the time of the Adoption of this Constitution, shall be eligible
to the Office of President; neither shall any Person be eligible to that
Office who shall not have attained to the Age of thirty-five Years, and
been fourteen Years a Resident within the United States.

[In Case of the Removal of the President from Office, or of his
Death, Resignation, or Inability to discharge the Powers and Duties
of the said Office, the same shall devolve on the Vice President, and
the Congress may by Law provide for the Case of Removal, Death,
Resignation or Inability, both of the President and Vice President,
declaring what Officer shall then act as President, and such Officer
shall act accordingly, until the Disability be removed, or a President
shall be elected.][7]

---

6   Changed by the Twelfth Amendment
7   Changed by the Twenty-Fifth Amendment

The President shall, at stated Times, receive for his Services, a Compensation, which shall neither be increased nor diminished during the Period for which he shall have been elected, and he shall not receive within that Period any other Emolument from the United States, or any of them.

Before he enter on the Execution of his Office, he shall take the following Oath or Affirmation:

"I do solemnly swear (or affirm) that I will faithfully execute the Office of President of the United States, and will to the best of my Ability, preserve, protect and defend the Constitution of the United States."

SECTION 2. The President shall be Commander in Chief of the Army and Navy of the United States, and of the Militia of the several States, when called into the actual Service of the United States; he may require the Opinion, in writing, of the principal Officer in each of the executive Departments, upon any subject relating to the Duties of their respective Offices, and he shall have Power to Grant Reprieves and Pardons for Offenses against the United States, except in Cases of Impeachment.

He shall have Power, by and with the Advice and Consent of the Senate, to make Treaties, provided two thirds of the Senators present concur; and he shall nominate, and by and with the Advice and Consent of the Senate, shall appoint Ambassadors, other public Ministers and Consuls, Judges of the supreme Court, and all other Officers of the United States, whose Appointments are not herein otherwise provided for, and which shall be established by Law: but the Congress may by Law vest the Appointment of such inferior Officers, as they think proper, in the President alone, in the Courts of Law, or in the Heads of Departments.

The President shall have Power to fill up all Vacancies that may happen during the Recess of the Senate, by granting Commissions which shall expire at the End of their next Session.

SECTION 3. He shall from time to time give to the Congress Information of the State of the Union, and recommend to their Consideration such Measures as he shall judge necessary and expedient; he may, on extraordinary Occasions, convene both Houses, or either of them, and in Case of Disagreement between them, with Respect to the Time of Adjournment, he may adjourn them to such Time as he shall think proper; he shall receive Ambassadors and other public Ministers; he shall take Care that the Laws be faithfully executed, and shall Commission all the Officers of the United States.

SECTION 4. The President, Vice President and all civil Officers of the United States, shall be removed from Office on Impeachment for, and Conviction of, Treason, Bribery, or other high Crimes and Misdemeanors.

Article III.

SECTION 1. The judicial Power of the United States, shall be vested in one supreme Court, and in such inferior Courts as the Congress may from time to time ordain and establish. The Judges, both of the supreme and inferior Courts, shall hold their Offices during good Behavior, and shall, at stated Times, receive for their Services a Compensation which shall not be diminished during their Continuance in Office.

SECTION 2. The judicial Power shall extend to all Cases, in Law and Equity, arising under this Constitution, the Laws of the United States, and Treaties made, or which shall be made, under their Authority; to all Cases affecting Ambassadors, other public Ministers and Consuls; to all Cases of admiralty and maritime Jurisdiction; to Controversies to which the United States shall be a Party; to Controversies between two or more States; [between a

State and Citizens of another State;]⁸ between Citizens of different States; between Citizens of the same State claiming Lands under Grants of different States, [and between a State, or the Citizens thereof, and foreign States, Citizens or Subjects.]⁹

In all Cases affecting Ambassadors, other public Ministers and Consuls, and those in which a State shall be Party, the supreme Court shall have original Jurisdiction. In all the other Cases before mentioned, the supreme Court shall have appellate Jurisdiction, both as to Law and Fact, with such Exceptions, and under such Regulations as the Congress shall make.

The Trial of all Crimes, except in Cases of Impeachment, shall be by Jury; and such Trial shall be held in the State where the said Crimes shall have been committed; but when not committed within any State, the Trial shall be at such Place or Places as the Congress may by Law have directed.

SECTION 3. Treason against the United States, shall consist only in levying War against them, or in adhering to their Enemies, giving them Aid and Comfort. No Person shall be convicted of Treason unless on the Testimony of two Witnesses to the same overt Act, or on Confession in open Court.

The Congress shall have power to declare the Punishment of Treason, but no Attainder of Treason shall work Corruption of Blood, or Forfeiture except during the Life of the Person attainted.

Article IV.

SECTION 1. Full Faith and Credit shall be given in each State to the public Acts, Records, and judicial Proceedings of every other State. And the Congress may by general Laws prescribe the Manner in which such Acts, Records and Proceedings shall be proved, and the Effect thereof.

---

8   Changed by the Eleventh Amendment.
9   Ibid.

SECTION 2. The Citizens of each State shall be entitled to all
Privileges and Immunities of Citizens in the several States.

A Person charged in any State with Treason, Felony, or other Crime,
who shall flee from Justice, and be found in another State, shall on
demand of the executive Authority of the State from which he fled,
be delivered up, to be removed to the State having Jurisdiction of the
Crime.

[No Person held to Service or Labour in one State, under the Laws
thereof, escaping into another, shall, in Consequence of any Law or
Regulation therein, be discharged from such Service or Labour, But
shall be delivered up on Claim of the Party to whom such Service or
Labour may be due.]¹⁰

SECTION 3. New States may be admitted by the Congress into
this Union; but no new States shall be formed or erected within
the Jurisdiction of any other State; nor any State be formed by
the Junction of two or more States, or parts of States,without the
Consent of the Legislatures of the States concerned as well as of
the Congress.

The Congress shall have Power to dispose of and make all needful
Rules and Regulations respecting the Territory or other Property
belonging to the United States; and nothing in this Constitution shall
be so construed as to Prejudice any Claims of the United States, or of
any particular State.

SECTION 4. The United States shall guarantee to every State
in this Union a Republican Form of Government, and shall
protect each of them against Invasion; and on Application of the
Legislature, or of the Executive (when the Legislature cannot be
convened) against domestic Violence.

Article V.

The Congress, whenever two thirds of both Houses shall deem it

---

10   Changed by the Thirteenth Amendment.

necessary, shall propose Amendments to this Constitution, or, on the Application of the Legislatures of two thirds of the several States, shall call a Convention for proposing Amendments, which, in either Case, shall be valid to all Intents and Purposes, as part of this Constitution, when ratified by the Legislatures of three fourths of the several States, or by Conventions in three fourths thereof, as the one or the other Mode of Ratification may be proposed by the Congress; Provided that no Amendment which may be made prior to the Year One thousand eight hundred and eight shall in any Manner affect the first and fourth Clauses in the Ninth Section of the first Article; and that no State, without its Consent, shall be deprived of its equal Suffrage in the Senate.

Article VI.

All Debts contracted and Engagements entered into, before the Adoption of this Constitution, shall be as valid against the United States under this Constitution, as under the Confederation.

This Constitution, and the Laws of the United States which shall be made in Pursuance thereof; and all Treaties made, or which shall be made, under the Authority of the United States, shall be the supreme Law of the Land; and the Judges in every State shall be bound thereby, any Thing in the Constitution or Laws of any State to the Contrary notwithstanding.

The Senators and Representatives before mentioned, and the Members of the several State Legislatures, and all executive and judicial Officers, both of the United States and of the several States, shall be bound by Oath or Affirmation, to support this Constitution; but no religious Test shall ever be required as a Qualification to any Office or public Trust under the United States.

Article VII.

The Ratification of the Conventions of nine States, shall be sufficient for the Establishment of this Constitution between the States so ratifying the Same.

Done in Convention by the Unanimous Consent of the States present the Seventeenth Day of September in the Year of our Lord one thousand seven hundred and Eighty seven and of the Independence of the United States of America the Twelfth. In Witness whereof We have hereunto subscribed our Names.

G. Washington — President and deputy from Virginia

BILL OF RIGHTS

The first ten Amendments to the Constitution
Ratified December 15, 1791
Followed by 17 Amendments ratified over the last two centuries.

Amendment 1

Congress shall make no law respecting an establishment of religion, or prohibiting the free exercise thereof; or abridging the freedom of speech, or of the press; or the right of the people peaceably to assemble, and to petition the Government for a redress of grievances.

Amendment 2

A well regulated Militia, being necessary to the security of a free State, the right of the people to keep and bear Arms, shall not be infringed.

Amendment 3

No Soldier shall, in time of peace be quartered in any house, without the consent of the Owner, nor in time of war, but in a manner to be prescribed by law.

Amendment 4

The right of the people to be secure in their persons, houses, papers, and effects, against unreasonable searches and seizures, shall not be violated, and no Warrants shall issue, but upon probable cause, supported by Oath or affirmation, and particularly describing the place to be searched, and the persons or things to be seized.

Amendment 5

No person shall be held to answer for a capital, or otherwise infamous crime, unless on a presentment or indictment of a Grand Jury, except in cases arising in the land or naval forces, or in the Militia, when in actual service in time of War or public danger; nor shall any person be subject for the same offense to be twice put in jeopardy of life or limb; nor shall be compelled in any criminal case to be a witness against himself, nor be deprived of life, liberty, or property, without due process of law; nor shall private property be taken for public use, without just compensation.

Amendment 6

In all criminal prosecutions, the accused shall enjoy the right to a speedy and public trial, by an impartial jury of the State and district wherein the crime shall have been committed, which district shall have been previously ascertained by law, and to be informed of the nature and cause of the accusation; to be confronted with the witnesses against him; to have compulsory process for obtaining witnesses in his favor, and to have the Assistance of Counsel for his defence.

Amendment 7

In Suits at common law, where the value in controversy shall exceed twenty dollars, the right of trial by jury shall be preserved, and no fact tried by a jury, shall be otherwise re-examined in any Court of the United States, than according to the rules of the common law.

Amendment 8

Excessive bail shall not be required, nor excessive fines imposed, nor cruel and unusual punishments inflicted.

Amendment 9

The enumeration in the Constitution, of certain rights, shall not be construed to deny or disparage others retained by the people.

Amendment 10

The powers not delegated to the United States by the Constitution, nor prohibited by it to the States, are reserved to the States respectively, or to the people.

AMENDMENT 11 – Ratified February 7, 1795.

The Judicial power of the United States shall not be construed to extend to any suit in law or equity, commenced or prosecuted against one of the United States by Citizens of another State, or by Citizens or Subjects of any Foreign State.

AMENDMENT 12 – Ratified June 15, 1804.

The Electors shall meet in their respective states and vote by ballot for President and Vice-President, one of whom, at least, shall not be an inhabitant of the same state with themselves; they shall name in their ballots the person voted for as President, and in distinct ballots the person voted for as Vice-President, and they shall make distinct lists of all persons voted for as President, and of all persons voted for as Vice-President, and of the number of votes for each, which lists they shall sign and certify, and transmit sealed to the seat of the government of the United States, directed to the President of the Senate; -- the President of the Senate shall, in the presence of the Senate and House of Representatives, open all the certificates and the votes shall then be counted; -- The person having the greatest number of votes for President, shall be the President, if such number be a majority of the whole number of Electors appointed; and if no person have such majority, then from the persons having the highest numbers not exceeding three on the list of those voted for as President, the House of Representatives shall choose immediately, by ballot, the President. But in choosing the President, the votes shall be taken by states, the representation from each state having one vote; a quorum for this purpose shall consist of a member or members from two-thirds of the states, and a majority of all the states shall be necessary to a choice. [And if the House of Representatives shall not choose a President whenever the right of choice shall devolve upon them, before the fourth day of March next following, then the Vice-President shall act as President, as in case of the death or other constitutional disability of the President. --][11]* The person having the greatest number of votes as Vice-President, shall be the Vice-President, if such number be a majority of the whole number of Electors appointed, and if no person have a majority, then from the two highest numbers on the list, the Senate shall choose the Vice-President; a quorum for the purpose shall consist of two-thirds of the whole number of Senators, and a majority of the whole number shall be necessary to a choice. But no person constitutionally ineligible to the office of President shall be eligible to that of Vice-President of the United States.

AMENDMENT 13 - Ratified December 6, 1865.

Section 1. Neither slavery nor involuntary servitude, except as a punishment for crime whereof the party shall have been duly convicted, shall exist within the United States, or any place subject to their jurisdiction.

Section 2. Congress shall have power to enforce this article by appropriate legislation.

AMENDMENT 14 - Ratified July 9, 1868.

Section 1. All persons born or naturalized in the United States, and subject to the jurisdiction thereof, are citizens of the United States and of the State wherein they reside. No State shall make or enforce any law which shall abridge the privileges or immunities of citizens of the United States; nor shall any State deprive any person of life, liberty, or property, without due process of law; nor deny to any person within its jurisdiction the equal protection of the laws.

Section 2. Representatives shall be apportioned among the several States according to their respective numbers, counting the whole number of persons in each State, excluding Indians not taxed. But when the right to vote at any election for the choice of electors for President and Vice-President of the United States, Representatives in Congress,

---

11   *Superseded by section 3 of the 20th amendment.

the Executive and Judicial officers of a State, or the members of the
Legislature thereof, is denied to any of the male inhabitants of such State,
being twenty-one years of age,[12] and citizens of the United States, or in
any way abridged, except for participation in rebellion, or other crime,
the basis of representation therein shall be reduced in the proportion
which the number of such male citizens shall bear to the whole number
of male citizens twenty-one years of age in such State.

Section 3. No person shall be a Senator or Representative in Congress,
or elector of President and Vice-President, or hold any office, civil or
military, under the United States, or under any State, who, having
previously taken an oath, as a member of Congress, or as an officer of the
United States, or as a member of any State legislature, or as an executive
or judicial officer of any State, to support the Constitution of the United
States, shall have engaged in insurrection or rebellion against the same,
or given aid or comfort to the enemies thereof. But Congress may by a
vote of two-thirds of each House, remove such disability.

Section 4. The validity of the public debt of the United States,
authorized by law, including debts incurred for payment of pensions and
bounties for services in suppressing insurrection or rebellion, shall not
be questioned. But neither the United States nor any State shall assume
or pay any debt or obligation incurred in aid of insurrection or rebellion
against the United States, or any claim for the loss or emancipation of
any slave; but all such debts, obligations and claims shall be held illegal
and void.

Section 5. The Congress shall have the power to enforce, by appropriate
legislation, the provisions of this article.

AMENDMENT 15 – Ratified February 3, 1870.

Section 1. The right of citizens of the United States to vote shall not be
denied or abridged by the United States or by any State on account of
race, color, or previous condition of servitude--

Section 2. The Congress shall have the power to enforce this article by
appropriate legislation.

---

12   *Changed by section 1 of the 26th amendment.

AMENDMENT 16 – Ratified February 3, 1913.

The Congress shall have power to lay and collect taxes on incomes, from whatever source derived, without apportionment among the several States, and without regard to any census or enumeration.

AMENDMENT 17 – Ratified April 8, 1913.

The Senate of the United States shall be composed of two Senators from each State, elected by the people thereof, for six years; and each Senator shall have one vote. The electors in each State shall have the qualifications requisite for electors of the most numerous branch of the State legislatures.

When vacancies happen in the representation of any State in the Senate, the executive authority of such State shall issue writs of election to fill such vacancies: Provided, That the legislature of any State may empower the executive thereof to make temporary appointments until the people fill the vacancies by election as the legislature may direct.

This amendment shall not be so construed as to affect the election or term of any Senator chosen before it becomes valid as part of the Constitution.

AMENDMENT 18 – Ratified January 16, 1919, repealed by amendment 21.

Section 1. After one year from the ratification of this article the manufacture, sale, or transportation of intoxicating liquors within, the importation thereof into, or the exportation thereof from the United States and all territory subject to the jurisdiction thereof for beverage purposes is hereby prohibited.

Section 2. The Congress and the several States shall have concurrent power to enforce this article by appropriate legislation.

Section 3. This article shall be inoperative unless it shall have been ratified as an amendment to the Constitution by the legislatures of the several States, as provided in the Constitution, within seven years from the date of the submission hereof to the States by the Congress.

AMENDMENT 19 – Ratified August 18, 1920.

The right of citizens of the United States to vote shall not be denied or abridged by the United States or by any State on account of sex.

Congress shall have power to enforce this article by appropriate legislation.

AMENDMENT 20 – Ratified January 23, 1933.

Section 1. The terms of the President and the Vice President shall end at noon on the 20th day of January, and the terms of Senators and Representatives at noon on the 3d day of January, of the years in which such terms would have ended if this article had not been ratified; and the terms of their successors shall then begin.

Section 2. The Congress shall assemble at least once in every year, and such meeting shall begin at noon on the 3d day of January, unless they shall by law appoint a different day.

Section 3. If, at the time fixed for the beginning of the term of the President, the President elect shall have died, the Vice President elect shall become President. If a President shall not have been chosen before the time fixed for the beginning of his term, or if the President elect shall have failed to qualify, then the Vice President elect shall act as President until a President shall have qualified; and the Congress may by law provide for the case wherein neither a President elect nor a Vice President shall have qualified, declaring who shall then act as President, or the manner in which one who is to act shall be selected, and such person shall act accordingly until a President or Vice President shall have qualified.

Section 4. The Congress may by law provide for the case of the death of any of the persons from whom the House of Representatives may choose a President whenever the right of choice shall have devolved upon them, and for the case of the death of any of the persons from whom the Senate may choose a Vice President whenever the right of choice shall have devolved upon them.

Section 5. Sections 1 and 2 shall take effect on the 15th day of October following the ratification of this article.

Section 6. This article shall be inoperative unless it shall have been ratified as an amendment to the Constitution by the legislatures of three-fourths of the several States within seven years from the date of its submission.

AMENDMENT 21 – Ratified December 5, 1933.

Section 1. The eighteenth article of amendment to the Constitution of the United States is hereby repealed.

Section 2. The transportation or importation into any State, Territory, or Possession of the United States for delivery or use therein of intoxicating liquors, in violation of the laws thereof, is hereby prohibited.

Section 3. This article shall be inoperative unless it shall have been ratified as an amendment to the Constitution by conventions in the several States, as provided in the Constitution, within seven years from the date of the submission hereof to the States by the Congress.

AMENDMENT 22 – Ratified February 27, 1951.

Section 1. No person shall be elected to the office of the President more than twice, and no person who has held the office of President, or acted as President, for more than two years of a term to which some other person was elected President shall be elected to the office of President more than once. But this Article shall not apply to any person holding the office of President when this Article was proposed by Congress, and shall not prevent any person who may be holding the office of President, or acting as President, during the term within which this Article becomes operative from holding the office of President or acting as President during the remainder of such term.

Section 2. This article shall be inoperative unless it shall have been ratified as an amendment to the Constitution by the legislatures of three-fourths of the several States within seven years from the date of its submission to the States by the Congress.

AMENDMENT 23 – Ratified March 29, 1961.

Section 1. The District constituting the seat of Government of the United States shall appoint in such manner as Congress may direct:

A number of electors of President and Vice President equal to the whole number of Senators and Representatives in Congress to which the District would be entitled if it were a State, but in no event more than the least populous State; they shall be in addition to those appointed by the States, but they shall be considered, for the purposes of the election of President and Vice President, to be electors appointed by a State; and they shall meet in the District and perform such duties as provided by the twelfth article of amendment.

Section 2. The Congress shall have power to enforce this article by appropriate legislation.

AMENDMENT 24 – Ratified January 23, 1964.

Section 1. The right of citizens of the United States to vote in any primary or other election for President or Vice President, for electors for President or Vice President, or for Senator or Representative in Congress, shall not be denied or abridged by the United States or any State by reason of failure to pay poll tax or other tax.

Section 2. The Congress shall have power to enforce this article by appropriate legislation.

AMENDMENT 25 – Ratified February 10, 1967.

Section 1. In case of the removal of the President from office or of his death or resignation, the Vice President shall become President.

Section 2. Whenever there is a vacancy in the office of the Vice President, the President shall nominate a Vice President who shall take office upon confirmation by a majority vote of both Houses of Congress.

Section 3. Whenever the President transmits to the President pro tempore of the Senate and the Speaker of the House of Representatives his written declaration that he is unable to discharge the powers and duties of his office, and until he transmits to them a written declaration to the contrary, such powers and duties shall be discharged by the Vice President as Acting President.

Section 4. Whenever the Vice President and a majority of either the principal officers of the executive departments or of such other body as Congress may by law provide, transmit to the President pro tempore of the Senate and the Speaker of the House of Representatives their written declaration that the President is unable to discharge the powers and duties of his office, the Vice President shall immediately assume the powers and duties of the office as Acting President.

Thereafter, when the President transmits to the President pro tempore of the Senate and the Speaker of the House of Representatives his written declaration that no inability exists, he shall resume the powers and duties of his office unless the Vice President and a majority of either the principal officers of the executive department or of such other body as Congress may by law provide, transmit within four days to the President pro tempore of the Senate and the Speaker of the House of Representatives their written declaration that the President is unable to discharge the powers and duties of his office. Thereupon Congress shall decide the issue, assembling within forty-eight hours for that purpose if not in session. If the Congress, within twenty-one days after receipt of the latter written declaration, or, if Congress is not in session, within twenty-one days after Congress is required to assemble, determines by two-thirds vote of both Houses that the President is unable to discharge the powers and duties of his office, the Vice President shall continue to discharge the same as Acting President; otherwise, the President shall resume the powers and duties of his office.

AMENDMENT 26 – Ratified July 1, 1971.

Section 1. The right of citizens of the United States, who are eighteen years of age or older, to vote shall not be denied or abridged by the United States or by any State on account of age.

Section 2. The Congress shall have power to enforce this article by appropriate legislation.

AMENDMENT 27 – Ratified May 7, 1992.

No law, varying the compensation for the services of the Senators and Representatives, shall take effect, until an election of representatives shall have intervened.

SUGGESTED RESOURCES

CONSTITUTION & DECLARATION

How to Read the Constitution and the Declaration of Independence, by Paul B. Skousen

The Making of America, by W. Cleon Skousen

The Debates of the Federal Convention of 1787, by James Madison

The Heritage Guide to the Constitution, by the Heritage Foundation

The Evolution and Destruction of the Original Electoral College, by Gary and Carolyn Alder

The Federalist Papers, Madison, et al

The Real George Washington, by Jay A. Perry

The Real Thomas Jefferson, by Andrew M. Allison

The Real Benjamin Franklin, Volume 1 and 2, by Andrew M. Allison, W. Cleon Skousen, and M. Richard Maxfield

Our Lost Constitution, by Mike Lee

The Liberty Amendments, by Mark Levin

The American Constitution—Its Origins and Development, by A. H. Kelly and W. A. Harbison

PRINCIPLES OF FREEDOM

The Law, by Frederic Bastiat

The 5000 Year Leap, by W. Cleon Skousen

The Naked Communist, by W. Cleon Skousen

It's Coming to America—The Majesty of God's Law, by W. Cleon Skousen

The Naked Socialist, by Paul B. Skousen

Two Treaties of Government, John Locke

An Essay Concerning Human Understanding, John Locke

Atlas Shrugged, by Ayn Rand

Anthem, by Ayn Rand

Liberty Defined, by Ron Paul

Democracy in America, by Alexis de Tocqueville

The Constitution of Liberty, by F. A. Hayek

Human Action, by Ludwig von Mises

The Ethics of Liberty, by Murray N. Rothbard

The Road to Serfdom, by F. A. Hayek

Understanding Crime and Gun-Control Laws, by John R. Lott Jr.

RELIGIOUS HISTORY OF AMERICA

The Bible, King James Version

It's Coming to America—The Majesty of God's Law, by W. Cleon Skousen

Christianity and the Constitution—The Faith of Our Founding Fathers, by John Eidsmoe

The Myth of Separation, by David Barton

In God We Trust, by Norman Cousins

FREE MARKET

The Wealth of Nations, by Adam Smith

The Free Market Reader: Essay in the Economics of Liberty, by Llewellyn H. Rockwell, ed.

Capitalism and Freedom, and
  Freedom to Choose, by Milton
  Friedman
Economics in One Lesson, by Henry
  Hazlitt
A Theory of Socialism and Capitalism,
  by Hans-Hermann Hoppe
*Basic Economics: A Citizens Guide to
  the Economy*, by Thomas Sowell

STUDIES IN ANTI-FREEDOM
Liberalism, by Ludwig von Mises
The Naked Capitalist, by W. Cleon
  Skousen
*The Creature from Jekyll Island—
  A Second Look at the Federal
  Reserve*, by G. Edward Griffin
1984, by George Orwell
Animal Farm, by George Orwell
Fahrenheit 451, by Ray Bradbury
Lord of the Flies, by William Golding

MOVIES, MEDIA
A More Perfect Union (1989 TV film,
  112 minutes)
The Crossing (2000 TV film, 89
  minutes)
Ten Secrets to a Best Seller (self
  publishing), by Tim McConnehey

FREEDOM ORGANIZATIONS
Heritage Foundation
Hillsdale College
Ludwig von Mises Institute
National Center For Constitutional
  Studies
 —among many others

ENDNOTES

NOTE: When W. Cleon Skousen passed away in 2006 he left behind a large body of works both published and still in draft form. With his permission, excerpts and summaries of his writings on certain concepts are included in the preceding text. They are drawn from:

> *The Naked Communist*
> *The 5000 Year Leap*
> *The Making of America*
> *It's Coming to America—The Majesty of God's Law*
> *Days of the Living Christ, Vol. I and II*
> *The Third Thousand Years*
> As well as his assorted notes, speeches, and commentaries

AUTHOR'S PREFACE

For an excellent discussion on the concepts of patriotism and love of country as provided in the *Federalist*, see Holmes Alexander's *How to Read the Federalist*.

PAGE V QUOTES

1   **Madison** quote: "I believe there are more instances ..." *History of the Virginia Federal Convention of 1788*, vol. 1, p. 130 (H.B. Grigsby ed. 1890).
    Lincoln quote: Sometimes given incorrectly as "We, the People are the rightful masters of both Congress and the courts — not to overthrow the Constitution, but to overthrow men who pervert the Constitution," stands corrected on page V, from a speech at Cincinnati, Ohio, September 17, 1859, see *The Papers And Writings of Abraham Lincoln, Volume Five, Constitution Edition*.
    Reagan quote: "Freedom is a fragile thing ...", Ronald Reagan Inaugural Address (as California Governor), January 5, 1967.

2   Thomas Jefferson quote: "If the freedom of religion, guaranteed to us by law in theory, can ever rise in practice under the overbearing inquisition of public opinion, truth will prevail over fanaticism, and the genuine doctrines of Jesus, so long perverted by His pseudo-priests, will again be restored to their original purity. This reformation will advance with the other improvements of the human mind,

but too late for me to witness it." Thomas Jefferson to Jared Sparks, November 4, 1820,reprinted in *Ethics an International Journal of Social, Political, and Legal Philosophy*, Vol. LIV, October 1943 No. i.

3   Speech by Fred G. Clark, Chairman of the American Economic Foundation—slightly edited due to space constraints. See full speech in *Congressional Record—Senate*, May 7, 1952, pp. 4868-4870.

4   Thomas Jefferson to Samuel Kercheval, 1816.

5   Alexander Hamilton quote: "Nothing is more common ...", from Phocion to the Considerate Citizens of New York, January 1-27, 1784."

6   See *The Declaration of Independence*.

7   J. Edgar Hoover quote: "Too often in recent years ...", remarks upon receiving the George Washington Award of Freedoms Foundation at Valley Forge, Pa., February 22, 1962; see *FBI Law Enforcement Bulletin*, Vol. 31, No. 4 April 1962.

8   Hoover quote: "...nation which honors God ..." *Congressional Record—House*, July 26, 1967, p. 20283.

9   See the *Declaration of Independence*.

10 Leonard E. Read quote: "...We cannot preserve ...", *Elements of Libertarian Leadership*, p. 17.

11 "Just start" was a life-long theme of David O. McKay, president of the Church of Jesus Christ of Latter-day Saints, restated privately to W. Cleon Skousen on the challenging subject of how to save the Constitution, December 1965.

12 Distilled from Parley P. Pratt, 1853, *Journal of Discourses* 1:139.

13 Group dynamics: Natural leaders or project initiators numbering 3–4% or fewer in large groups engaged in philanthropic activities was first suggested by Ezra T. Benson.

14 Isaiah 29:21.

15 The Eight Injurious Amendments—Some of the main controversies surrounding these Amendments include:
    #14: The imposition of the federal Bill of Rights on the states is used by the Supreme Court to informally repeal the

10th Amendment and to overturn states on social issues such as abortion, marriage, religion in public schools, display of the Ten Commandments, and so on; So-called "anchor babies."

#16: Violated states' right to give equal protection to its citizens (for example, graduated income taxes).

#17: This broke the linkage of representation by removing the state legislatures' right to hire/fire their own representatives (the Senators).

#18: Federal government crossed its constitutional boundary into states' rights to control alcohol, and was correctly repealed.

#22: The Framers wanted the voters to decide term limits, not the law.

#23: Giving Washington D.C. the rights and powers reserved to the states is a dangerous precedent that stacks political power in favor of one party. Who's next? NY, LA, Chicago? Better to let D.C. residents vote in Maryland from where D.C. was originally carved out.

#25: Allows unelected appointees to occupy the office of President and Vice President (example: Ford and Rockefeller). A better approach is to have a 3/4ths majority vote by Congress so that more parts of nation are included in the decision, not just the majority party in power.

#26: A lower voting age remains controversial because of issues of maturity, judgment, and increased susceptibility to emotional compromise for political gain.

16 James Madison quote: "That which is least imperfect ...", Madison to unknown, 1833, Hunt 9:528.

17 For more information about the rise and fall of nations due to corruption and their adopting socialistic forms, see *The Naked Socialist,* by Paul B. Skousen.

18 Henning W. Prentis, Jr., February 1943 speech, "The Cult of Competency," see *The General Magazine and Historical Chronicle*, Vol. XLV, Numb. III, April 1943, pp. 272-73.

19 Ibid., Skousen, *The Naked Socialist*.

20 Matthew 13:45-46.

21 Quote from Fred G. Clark, Chairman of the American Economic Foundation, *Congressional Record, Senate*, May 7, 1952 pp. 4870.

22 Albert E. Bowen, *Conference Reports*, October 1944, pp. 153-158.

23 Charles Pinckney quote: "Is there at this moment ...", Jonathan Elliot, ed., *The Debates in the Several State Conventions, on the Adoption of the Federal Constitution*, Vol. 4, Philadelphia: J.B. Lippincott and Company, pp. 318.

24 Charles Pinckney quote: "To fraud, to force ...", Ibid., Jonathan Elliot, ed., p. 318.

25 James Madison quote: "The accumulation of all powers ...", *Federalist* No. 47.

26 Thomas Jefferson quote: "The concentrating these in ...", Jefferson, *Notes on Virginia*.

27 Thomas Jefferson, *The Works of Thomas Jefferson*, 7:223.

28 Albert E. Bowen quote: "That which is right ..." *Conference Reports*, April 1941, p. 85.

29 James Wilson describes these very pyramids in *Commentaries on the Constitution of the United States of America*, James Wilson and Thomas M'Kean, 1792, p. 130.

30 William Blackstone quote: "No matter how abandoned ..." William Blackstone, *Commentaries on the Laws of England*, 1:119–23, 1765.

31 Thomas Jefferson quote: "What country can preserve ...", *Works* 2:318.

32 See *The Declaration of Independence*, opening sentence.

33 Wood, *The Creation of the American Republic*, op. cit., p. 68.

34 Albert E. Bowen quote: "When there is a ..." *Conference Report*, October, 1948 p. 87.

35 Washington quote: "The general government ...", *Writings of George Washington*, 11:219.

36 Ibid.

37 Bergh, *The Writings of Thomas Jefferson*, op. cit., 14:198.

38 John Adams quote: "general principles," Adams to Thomas Jefferson, Bergh, *The Writings of Thomas Jefferson*, 13:293.

39 Samuel Adams quote: "… the religion of America …" Wells, *Life of Samuel Adams*, 3:23.

40 *The Annals of America* (22 volume set), op. cit., 3:612.

41 See "What is a Right" in *The Naked Socialist*, Paul B. Skousen.

42 Blackstone, *Commentaries on the Laws of England*, op. cit., p. 40 in the original at top of the page; in the Jones ed. pp. 59-62 at the bottom of the page.

43 Ibid., p. 42 in the original at the top of the page; in the Jones ed., p. 64 at the bottom of the page.

44 Madison, *Federalist* No. 46.

45 *The Annals of America*, op. cit., 2:447-448.

46 John Locke, *Second Essay Concerning Civil Government*, p. 47, par. 96-97.

47 The precise number of powers granted to Congress varies depending on how the list is read. As a list of clauses there are 18 powers. Identifying powers not strongly linked to each other can increase the count. For example, separating out "paying debts" from Clause 1 totals 19 powers. Separating out "bankruptcies" from Clause 4, and separating out "weights and measures" from Clause 5 brings the total to 21. Other clauses can be similarly parsed, but for the convenience of general reference, we round it out at 20 powers.

48 "Why the President Said No," in Essays on Liberty, 12 vols., The Foundation for Economic Education, Inc., 1952-1965, 3:255.

49 Locke, *Second Essay Concerning Civil Government*, op. cit., 35:46-47.

50   Ibid., 35:48.
51   Bergh, *The Writings of Thomas Jefferson*, op cit., 14:421.
52   Locke, *Second Essay Concerning Civil Government*, op. cit., 35:37.
53   Madison, *Federalist* No. 57.
54   John Adams, Dissertation on the Canon and the Federal Law, February 1765, and quoted by Koch in *The American Enlightenment*, op. cit., p. 239.
55   Smyth, *The Writings of Benjamin Franklin*, op. cit., 2:347.
56   Fitzpatrick, *Writings of George Washington*, op. cit., 30:491.
57   Bergh, *The Writings of Thomas Jefferson*, op. cit., 3:321.
58   Ibid., 35:233.
59   1 Corinthians 11:11.
60   A letter to a young friend on June 25, 1745, and quoted by Koch in *The American Enlightenment*, op. cit., p. 70.
61   John Locke, *The Second Essay Concerning Civil Government*, p. 37, par. 58.
62   Alexis de Tocqueville, *Democracy in America*, op. cit., 1:315.
63   Ibid., 13:357-358.
64   Quoted by Cherry in *God's New Israel*, op. cit., p. 65.
65   Bergh, *The Writings of Thomas Jefferson*, op. cit., 10:217.
66   Hamilton, *Federalist* No. 1.
67   Madison, *Federalist* No. 14.
68   Lord Acton quoted: "Liberty is not the power," The Roman Question, published in the *Rambler*, 1860, quoted in Fears 1988, 613.
69   Clinton Rossiter quote: "A thorough check of newspapers ..." *Seedtime of the Republic: The Origin of the American Tradition of Political Liberty*, by Clinton Rossiter, New York: Harcourt, Brace and Company, 1953.
70   John Adams quote: "...rage for profit and commerce ..." John Adams to Mercy Warren, January 8, 1776.
71   Thomas Paine, *Common Sense—Of the Present Ability of America: with some Miscellaneous Reflections*, para. 19, third edition, February 14, 1776: "...It might be difficult, if not impossible, to form the Continent into one government half a century hence. ..."
72   Richard Bushman quote: "...there was nothing reassuring to the framers ..." Richard L. Bushman, Virtue and the Constitution, published in *By the Hands of Wise Men: Essays on the U.S. Constitution*, Provo, Utah, Brigham Young University Press, 1979.
73   Richard Bushman, Virtue and the Constitution, published in *By the Hands of Wise Men: Essays on the U.S. Constitution*, Provo, Utah, Brigham Young University Press, 1979.
74   Lord Acton quote: "Men cannot be made good by the state ..." *Selected Writings of Lord Acton*, Vol. 3, Add. mss. 4939, p. 3, Liberty Fund 1988.
75   Benjamin Franklin quote: "Only a virtuous people are capable ..." Smyth, *Writings of Benjamin Franklin*, 9:569.
76   Richard Henry Lee quote: "It is certainly true that ..." Richard Henry Lee to Martin Pickett March 5, 1786.
77   Wells, Life of Samuel Adams, 3:175.
78   John Adams, letter to Zabdiel Adams, June 21, 1776.
79   Samuel Williams, *A Discourse on the Love of Our Country*, Salem, 1775, pp 13–14.
80   George Washington, First Inaugural Address, April 30, 1789.
81   Letter to George Chapman, Dec. 15, 1784.
82   Quoted in Adrienne Koch, ed., *The American Enlightenment*, George Braziller, New York, 1965, p. 77.
83   Ford, *Writings of Thomas Jefferson*, p. 227.
84   John Adams, Diary, June 2, 1778.
85   Proverbs 22:6.
86   Jared Sparks, *The Works of Benjamin Franklin*, 1882, p. 48.
87   George Washington, First Inaugural Address, April 30, 1789.
88   Thomas Jefferson, Westmoreland County Petition, November 2, 1785.
89   Thomas Jefferson to James Sullivan, May 21, 1805.
90   Thomas Jefferson quote: "Dependence begets subservience ..." Thomas Jefferson *Notes on the State of Virginia*, Query XIX, 1787.
91   John Witherspoon quote: "Nothing is more certain than a general profligacy ..." The Dominion of Providence Over the Passions of Men, a sermon at Princeton, May 17, 1776.
92   Quoted in Jonathan Elliot, ed., *The Debates in the Several State Conventions on the Adoption of the Federal Constitution*, 5 vols., J. B. Lippincott Company.
93   John Adams quote: "Public virtue cannot exist ..." John Adams to Mercy Warren April 16, 1776.
94   George Washington, circular letter of farewell to the Army, June 8, 1783.
95   Abraham Lincoln quote: "Let every American ...", Address Before the Young Men's Lyceum of Springfield, Illinois, January 27, 1838.
96   This phrase comes from The Book of Alma 37:6-7, and encompasses the idea of a grain of mustard seed or doing small works that bring about great things, such as the concepts expressed in Matthew 17:20, Isaiah 41:10-13, Luke 17:6, Romans 8:28, Matthew 25:11, Matthew 6:33, Galatians 5:9, Luke 16:10 & 18:27, and so forth.
97   *Declaration of Independence*, second paragraph.
98   A variation on the statement by George Santayana (Spain, 1863-1952), "Those who cannot remember the past are condemned to repeat it," from *The Life of Reason: The Phases of Human Progress*, Vol. I, *Reason in Common Sense*, (1905-1906).
99   For more information about living a common, universal moral code, see *The*

5000 Year Leap, by W. Cleon Skousen.

100 Daniel Webster quote: "The Bible is a book which teaches ...", "And it is not be be doubted ..." Daniel Webster, Address Delivered at Bunker Hill, June 17, 1843, on the Completion of the Monument (Boston: T. R. Marvin, 1843), p. 31. See also W. P. Strickland, *History of the American Bible Society from its Organization to the Present Time,* New York: Harper and Brothers, 1849, p. 18.

101 Noah Webster quote: "All the ... evils which men suffer ..." History of the United States, Noah Webster, 1832, p. 339.

102 Dr. Benjamin Rush, *A Defence of the Use of the Bible in Schools,* from a tract published by the American Tract Society around1830.

103 For a more detailed discussion about the laws and statutes in ancient Israel, see W. Cleon Skousen, *It's Coming to America— The Majesty of God's Law,* Ensign Publishing, 2017.

104 Apostle Paul quote: "For if a man know not how to rule ..." 1 Timothy 3:5.

105 Edmund Burke quote: "Men are qualified ...", *Works of Edmund Burke,* 4:51-51.

106 Albert E. Bowen quote: "Right and wrong are moral ..." *Conference Reports,* October 1944, 153-158.

107 Gouverneur Morris quote: "There must be religion. ..." An Inaugural Discourse: Delivered Before the New York Historical Society," September 4, 1816.

108 Richard Henry Lee quote: "Refiners may weave as fine a web ..." Richard Henry Lee letter to James Madison, November 26, 1784.

109 John Adams Quote: "Our Constitution was made only for a moral ..." John Adams letter to Massachusetts Militia, October 11, 1798.

110 John Adams Quote: "The Bible is the best book ..." John Adams letter to Thomas Jefferson, December 25, 1813.

111 Samuel Adams quote: "... wisest constitution nor the wisest laws ..." from an essay published in *The Advertiser,* 1748, later reprinted in *The Life and Public Service of Samuel Adams,* Volume 1 (1865) by William Vincent Wells.

112 Thomas Jefferson quote: "And can the liberties of a nation ..." Thomas Jefferson, *Notes on the State of Virginia,* Query XVIII, edited by Peden, p. 163.

113 John Adams quote: "It is the duty of all men..." *The Works of John Adams,* Charles Francis Adams, vol. VI, Charles C. Little and James Brown publishers, 1851, p. 64.

114 James Madison quote: "In its larger and juster meaning ..." James Madison, *National Gazette,* March 27, 1792.

115 Ezra Taft Benson quote: "You can't do wrong and feel right." Ezra Taft Benson, Preparing Yourself for Missionary Service, April 1985.

116 George Washington to the United Baptist Churches of Virginia, May 1789.

117 George Washington to the General Assembly of the Presbyterian Church, May 30 to June 5, 1789.

118 Hayek quote: "...makes use of all men" F. A. Hayek, *Individualism and Economic Order,* p. 11.

119 George Washington, Farewell Address, September 19, 1796.

120 Charles Carroll: Letter to Secretary of War James McHenry, November 4, 1800.

121 W. Cleon Skousen, *It's Coming to America–The Majesty of God's Law,* Statutes, p. 561, Ensign Publishing, 2018.

122 Nations and peoples who enjoyed prolonged periods of peace by living natural law or God's Law include ancient Israel, remnants of the lost ten tribes of Israel in northern Europe where remnants of the Hebrew law were found in practice including Lowland Scotch, Normans, Danes, Norwegians, Swedes, Germans, Dutch, Belgians, Lombards, Franks, the Anglo-Saxons; and for a time, ancient Greece, and the Roman Republic. See W. Cleon Skousen, *It's Coming to America– The Majesty of God's Law,* Chapter 15, Ensign Publishing, 2017.

123 See *The Declaration of Independence* preamble that begins "When in the course..."

124 False witnesses punished with that which they hoped to mete out, see Deuteronomy 19:15-21.

125 Galatians 6:5-6 "... whatsoever a man soweth ..."

126 For an in-depth look at faith among the settlers and colonists of America, see *Christianity and the Constitution, The Faith of Our Founding Fathers,* John Eidsmoe, Baker Book House Company, 1987.

127 Thomas Jefferson quote: "The practice of morality being necessary ..." Thomas Jefferson to James Fishback (draft), September 27, 1809.

128 Patrick Henry quote: "Righteousness alone can exalt ..." *The Life of Patrick Henry,* S. G. Arnold, Hurst & Company Publishers, Chapter 4, p. 69.

129 Benjamin Franklin quote: "As to Jesus of Nazareth, ..." Benjamin Franklin to Ezra Stiles, March 9, 1790.

130 Joseph Story quote: "I verily believe that Christianity is ..." *Joseph Story, Life and Letters of Joseph Story,* William W. Story, editor (Boston: Charles C. Little and James Brown, 1851), Vol. I, p. 92, March 24, 1801.

131 George Washington quote: "The distinguished character of a Patriot, ..." Washington's General Orders, May 2, 1778.

132 George Washington quote: "You do well to wish to learn ..." George Washington Address to the Delaware Nation, May 12, 1779.

133 John Adams quote: "The Christian religion is, above all ..." John Adams Diaries (1750s-1790s), July 26, 1796.

134 John Hancock quote: "Sensible of the importance of Christian ..." Inaugural Address of John Hancock as Governor of Massachusetts, 1780.

135 John Quincy Adams quote: "In the chain of human events ..." Newburyport Oration, July 4, 1837.

136 Benjamin Rush quote: "...by renouncing the Bible ..." Benjamin Rush to John Adams, January 23, 1807.

137 Benjamin Rush quote: "The great enemy of salvation of man ..." Benjamin Rush open letter "To the citizens of Philadelphia: A plan for Free Schools," March 28, 1787.

138 Daniel Webster quote: "... to a free and universal reading of the Bible ..." Speech at the Bunker Hill Monument, June 17, 1843.

139 Noah Webster quote: "The moral and religious precepts ..." and "All the miseries and evils" written in the preface to *The American Dictionary of the English Language, 1828.*

140 Benjamin Rush quote: "The Bible contains more knowledge necessary ..." and "The Bible when not read in schools ..." A Defence of the Use of the Bible in Schools, Dr. Benjamin Rush, 1830.

141 Daniel and the lions' den, Daniel 6.

142 Shadrach, Meshach, and Abednego in the fiery furnace, see Daniel 2-3.

143 "Come unto me ..." Matthew 11:28-29.

144 Matthew 5:1-12, the Beatitudes.

145 Matthew 5:13-16.

146 Matthew 5:21-32.

147 Matthew 5:21-26.

148 Matthew 5:27-32.

149 Matthew 5:33-37.

150 Matthew 5:33-37.

151 Matthew 15:18.

152 Matthew 5:38-42.

153 No compensation possible or satisfaction acceptable for murder, see Numbers 35:31, and 16-18, 20-21; Deuteronomy 19:11-13.

154 See Amendments 4, 5, 6, 7, 8.

155 Matthew 5:43-48.

156 Matthew 7:12, Golden Rule.

157 Matthew 7:12, Golden Rule.

158 Matthew 6:8, Father knows beforehand.

159 Benjamin Franklin, "...in all cases of public service, the less profit, the greater the honor," oration delivered at the Constitutional Convention, June 2, 1787.

160 Matthew 7:1-6, Judge not unrighteously.

161 Matthew 7:7–11, Ask and knock.

162 Matthew 7:13–14, Strait gate.

163 Matthew 7:20, By their fruits ye shall know.

164 Matthew 7:15–20, Beware false prophets.

165 Thomas Jefferson to William Charles Jarvis, September 28, 1820.

166 Matthew 7:20, By their fruits.

167 Matthew 7:1–5, Judge not.

168 See *The Declaration of Independence.*

169 Matthew 7:24–28, Build house on rock.

170 This famous quote about choosing to be "governed by God or become ruled by tyrants" may be attributed to assorted authors including William Penn, Norman Vincent Peale, Roy Masters, David Barton, among others.

171 Long-standing estimates of pornography's financial standing of $10 billion to $14 billion in annual sales has been challenged as overrated. While it is lucrative and growing, evolving access has cut into its financial growth. See, for example, Dan Ackman, "How Big Is Porn?" Forbes, May 25, 2001. Accurate numbers are difficult to derive, and are still estimated to be around the $4 billion mark in the U.S. alone in 2018, but the enormity of the industry is unquestionably a devastating plague on the world.

172 Matthew 5:44: "But I say unto you, Love your enemies ..."

173 Matthew 5:39: "But I say unto you, That ye resist not evil but whosoever shall smite thee on they right cheek, turn to him the other also."

174 Luke 22:36: "Then said he unto them, But now, he that had a purse, let him take it, and likewise his scrip: and he that hath no sword, let him sell his garment, and buy one."

175 See, for example, Daniel Goleman, *Therapists See Religion as Aid, Not Illusion,* New York Times 1991; Michael E. McCullough, Brian L. B. Willoughby, *Religion, Self-Regulation, and Self-Control: Associations, Explanations, and Implications,* Psychological Bulletin 2009, Vol. 135, No. 1, 69-93; et al.

176 For more information about he importance of a written Constitution, see *The 5000 Year Leap,* by W. Cleon Skousen.

177 Fabian socialist's quote: "England's [unwritten] Constitution ..." *Introduction to The American Fabian,* 1895.

178 Ramsey MacDonald quote: "...road bloc to reform" *Fabian News,* February 1898.

179 See Paul B. Skousen, *The Naked Socialist,* chapter 15, Ensign Publishing Co., 2014.

180 Un-codified constitutions are not arranged into a single system or document; they are typically without formal written words and take their form from customs, a long history of precedent, usage and an evolving variety of documents, legal instruments, legislation passed anciently or recently, commentary by judges or experts; they are recognized by those in political power or the courts as binding on the government, often called "unwritten constitution," although some components may be written in whole or part. Being unwritten and/or un-codified they are highly elastic and therefore not very reliable and easily changed. Examples of nations with an un-codified constitution include the United Kingdom, Canada, Israel, New Zealand, Saudi Arabia.

181 Jack Straw quote: "The constitution of the United Kingdom exists ...", Independent online, February 14, 2008, *The Big Question: Why doesn't the UK have a written constitution, and does it matter?*

182 John Adams quote: "No man will contend ..." *Writings of John Adams* 4:403; cf. 4:401, 526.

183 Thomas Jefferson quote: "Our peculiar security is in ..." Thomas Jefferson letter to Carey Nicholas, September 7, 1803.

184 "Teach them correct principles ..." Joseph Smith Jr., quoted by John Taylor, *Millennial Star*, 15 Nov. 1851, p. 339.

185 John Locke quote: "The end of law ...", *Second Treatise of Government*, Ch. VI, sec. 57.

186 John Locke, ibid.

187 Copyright by Gene Roddenberry, and varying studios such as Desilu, Paramount Pictures, and a host of others in production and distribution that later attached to the Star Trek franchise.

188 Copyright by George Lucas, Lucasfilm, The Walt Disney Company, 20th Century Fox, and others involved in the production and distribution activities attached to the Star Wars franchise.

189 Paul B. Skousen, *How to Read the Constitution and the Declaration of Independence*, Izzard Ink Publishing, 2nd edition, 2017.

190 For a good description of how that process has ruined nations and peoples throughout history, see *The Naked Socialist* by Paul B. Skousen.

191 Benjamin Franklin on the dangers of a salaried bureaucracy, oration by Franklin in the Constitutional Convention, June 2, 1787.

192 J. Gordon Hylton, *How Much Difference Does the Small State Advantage in the Electoral College Really Make?* Marquette University Law School Faculty Blog, March 8, 2010.

193 The National Popular Vote Interstate Compact is an agreement among several states to award all their respective electoral votes to whichever candidate wins the overall popular vote in all 50 states and the District of Columbia. This process dilutes the ability of the small states to play a role using their "senate bump" advantage. Another effort at diluting influence is to enlarge the number of voting districts (House representatives) from the current 435 to 770 or more.

194 See 156 U.S. 51.

195 *Federalist* No. 49.

196 Birthright citizenship was debated by Congress, in particular regarding Chinese children born in California, gypsies, and other foreigners. See the comments of Sen. Jacob Howard, the author of the citizenship clause, in the *Congressional Globe*, May 30, 1866: "This will not, of course, include persons born in the United States who are foreigners, aliens, who belong to the families of ambassadors or foreign ministers accredited to the Government of the United States." The presence of deeply divided partisan interpretation is

evidence this section must be revisited and amended.

197 Originally from Joseph Smith Jr., "I teach them correct principles and they govern themselves," *Teachings of Presidents of the Church: Joseph Smith*, p. 284, 2007.

198 F. A. Harper quote: "Correct action...", F. A. Harper, *Liberty: A Path to Its Recovery*, p. 126.

199 See The Ten Commandments, #'s 8 and 10, the Book of Exodus 20:3-17.

200 James Madison quote: "Government is instituted ...", *Essay on Property*, 1792.

201 John Adams quote: "Property must be secured ...", John Adams, *Works*, 6:8-9.

202 Jefferson to Thomas Mann Randolph, May 30, 1790.

203 New York Times, December 26, 1964.

204 Salt Lake Tribune, October 26, 1985.

205 Much of the material for this section is influenced by Thomas G. West, *The Political Theory of the American Founding: Natural Rights, Public Policy, and the Moral Conditions of Freedom*, New York: Cambridge University Press, 2017.

206 James Madison quote: "Diversity in the faculties ...", see *Federalist* 10.

207 Fitzpatrick, *Writings of George Washington*, 11:217.

208 For sources and details about the Supreme Court rulings cited here, see *The Naked Socialist* by Paul B. Skousen, chapter 63; Ensign Publishing, 2014.

209 For sources and details mentioned here about the Federal Reserve, see *The Naked Capitalist* by W. Cleon Skousen, privately published in 1970.

210 For a more detailed explanation of fractional banking see *The Naked Capitalist*, and *The 5000 Year Leap*, both by W. Cleon Skousen.

211 Benjamin Franklin, *On the Price of Corn and Management of the Poor*, November 29, 1766.

212 For FY 2018, Social Security cost $988 billion, Medicare cost $589 billion, Medicaid cost $642 billion and other welfare programs were estimated at $449 billion. Pulling out Social Security and Medicare costs as returns on paycheck deductions leaves $1.1 trillion. Some 40 million are on food stamps. See: www.usgovernmentspending.com, and The United States Department of Agriculture.

213 See *Status of the Social Security and Medicare Programs, 2019*, at ssa.gov/

214 For sources and details about the union activities cited here see *The Naked Socialist* by Paul B. Skousen, chapter 58; Ensign Publishing, 2014.

215 See: www.FTC.gov/policy/advocacy/economic-liberty, accessed January 5, 2019.

216 Sam Adams to Massachusetts's agent in London, 1768.

217 Thomas Jefferson to Joseph Milligan, April 6, 1816.

218 John Adams, *A Defense of the Constitutions of Government of the United States of America*, 1787.

219 Thomas Jefferson, First Inaugural Address, March 4, 1801.

220 Thomas Jefferson to Thomas Cooper, November 29, 1802.

221 Thomas Jefferson to Albert Gallatin, June 16, 1817.

222 James Madison to James Robertson, April 20, 1825.

223 James Madison, 4 Annals of Congress 179, 1794.

224 James Madison speech at the House of Representatives, January 10, 1794.

225 Attributed to Benjamin Franklin; similar quote also attributed to Alexander Fraser Tytler.

226 James Madison, *Federalist* No. 58, February 20, 1788.

227 James Madison to Thomas Jefferson, October 17, 1788.

228 Thomas Jefferson to Charles Hammond, August 18, 1821.

229 James Madison to Edmund Pendleton, January 21, 1792.

230 James Madison, speech to the Virginia Ratifying Convention, June 16, 1788.

231 Benjamin Franklin in *On the Price of Corn and Management of the Poor*, Nov. 29, 1766.

232 Thomas Jefferson in *An Act for Establishing Religious Freedom*, passed in the Assembly of Virginia in the beginning of the year 1786.

233 John Adams to Abigail Adams, July 17, 1775.

234 Institute for Economic Freedom and Opportunity, annual report *Economic Freedom in America–2017*, The Heritage Foundation, Washington, DC.

235 Pew Survey of gains, losses, and household economic experiences, published March 9, 2017.

236 Experian *State of Credit: 2017*, published January 11, 2018.

237 "Lift where you stand," speech by Dieter F. Uchtdorf, General Conference of the Church of Jesus Christ of Latter-day Saints, October 2008.

DEDICATION: This book is fondly dedicated to my mother, Jewel P. Skousen, who turned 100 in August 2018, and was happy to apply to this text her beautiful gift of editing. And, to my father W. Cleon Skousen (1913-2006) whose lifetime of scholarship, faith, and enthusiasm brought to life and clarity the concepts in these pages. And, to Kathy, my bride of 43 years, whose inimitable loving patience never failed an all-too-often absentee husband whose longest hours were in the basement office at the keyboard while she was chief caregiver for Jewel, our household, and our own family of ten children and 38 grandchildren.—With great appreciation, respect, admiration, and love.

ABOUT THE AUTHORS

Paul B. Skousen is an investigative journalist, author, and teacher. He received his MA from Georgetown University and worked as an intelligence officer in the CIA and the White House. His books include *The Naked Socialist, How to Read the Constitution and the Declaration of Independence, Treasures from the Journal of Discourses*, a three-volume historical fiction series *Bassam and the Seven Secret Scrolls*, among others. He is a professor of communications and journalism.

Dr. W. Cleon Skousen (1913-2006) was a popular public speaker, teacher, and writer. He served as Chief of Police in Salt Lake City, and during his 16 years with the FBI he was an Agent, a communications sector administrator at FBI headquarters, and an authorized public speaker for Director J. Edgar Hoover. He received his Juris Doctor degree from George Washington University Law School. He authored dozens of books and founded The Freemen Institute and the National Center for Constitutional Studies. Through these organizations he taught constitutional history and principles to more than three million people over the span of 30 years. He has lectured in all 50 states and in more than 40 countries worldwide. His national bestsellers include *The Naked Communist, The Naked Capitalist, The 5000 Year Leap, The Making of America, It's Coming to America—The Majesty of God's Law*, among others.

INDEX